Potato Chip Leadership Skills

Fostering tools of success for those seeking to build their management, mentoring and growth in the sales world.

Written By
Kathy Burrows

Kirby Publishing, LLC
Lacey, WA 98503

ISBN (Paperback Form): 978-1-947863-07-1

ISBN (E-Book Form): 978-1-947863-09-5

Library of Congress Control Number:2019955306

Edited by Angela Bilancini.

Front cover image & book design by Troy Kirby.

Printed and bound in the United States of America.

First printing November 2019.

Published by Kirby Publishing, LLC

Lacey, WA 98503

Visit www.ticketsalesu.com for more information.

Foreword
By
Amy Scheer

We all know sports…

Most of us have played sports our entire lives and couldn't bare giving it up…hence our career choice.

Whether we participated in youth sports as children and teenagers in our athletic prime or as weekend warriors in adult leagues to get our competitive fix each week – we just can't get enough.

And given how much sports mirrors life, this is a good thing.

Sports teaches you so many life lessons but maybe the most important ones are work ethic, teamwork and leadership. So simple yet sometimes so difficult to incorporate into the daily management of your day and team.

Most often we learn these principles through our coach(es). It's so important that the coach leads their team with the right set of guiding principles.

How often do we love our coach, agree with our coach and want to bust our butt for the coach? When you find that perfect coach you want to run through a wall for them. Well I met that coach and her name is Kathy Burrows!

I had the privilege of working with Kathy Burrow- first at MSG – courtesy of Scott O'Neil. Scott was brave enough to allow the Liberty to hire their own ticket sales staff.

What did I know about ticket sales…well enough to set a foundation, but not enough to lead and mentor the team on a day to day basis. In came my own personal superhero – Kathy!!

From day one her coaching skills were evident…and she preached the same things daily:

- We plan for success

- We work as a team

- We take accountability for our actions

- We celebrate each other

- We execute at the highest level

I jumped on board the fast-moving Kathy train and took it all in. I am not sure she realized that as she was teaching our Account Executives, she was teaching me as well. With eyes and ears wide open I learned how to lead with empathy, fun… how to have the tough conversations along with the fun ones…how to develop high achieving team members…how to ensure that they learned from every situation. Her leadership and guidance led to unprecedented ticket sales success for the Liberty. We had our best years under her tutelage and leadership and I believe to this day it is all about her leadership style and the fact that we would all run through a wall for her.

Lucky for me she has become a personal friend and mentor – someone I talk to daily who guides me and continually works with me to grow as a mentor, leader and overall better human being.

Amy Scheer, Consultant to Madison Square Garden

Amy has held high profile sports positions including Vice President of Broadcasting, New Jersey Nets, Vice President of Marketing and Communications at MSG for the NY Liberty, Director of Marketing and Events at Grand Central Terminal NY, Vice President Marketing, Media and FRM NYCFC, Chief Commercial Officer New York Red Bulls, and her current Consultant to Madison Square Garden.

Editor's Note: Potato Chip Leaderskip Skills is as much as a training manual as a general sales management book read. That's why we've included several instances of white space between Kathy Burrow's various concepts, ideas and examples. It serves as a resource for ticket sales directors and managers to engage in training their own staff, using Potato Chip Leadership Skills, where new account representatives can jot down their own thoughts against the sales method primer within the pages of this text.

As I wrote this second book, I couldn't help but be appreciative to those who have carved the way for me...

My mom, Veronica Tokarczyk, the original leader. From raising 4 children, one with developmental challenges, as a single parent midway through her life, and yet still believing in each and every one of us and what we could accomplish. She kept encouraging me to take that chance.

To those who read my Potato Chip Ticket Sales, my blogs, Linkedin articles and tweets. Your support and quest to get better is what keeps me smiling every day.

To Alan Ledford and Brad Taylor of Mountain Star Sports who inspire me every time I go to El Paso with their outstanding leadership and their belief in each and every member of their team. They don't say they grow and develop. They do it. The best at what they do.

To Troy Kirby who continues to motivate me and inspire me to share what's in my head in writing. At this rate, I'll be writing 20 more books. Ok maybe one or two more!

To my wonderful editor, Angela Bilancini who surprisingly enjoys what I write and is great at understanding "kathyspeak"

And of course to my kids, David, Michael and Anne. Being your mom has been the best leadership job I've been given. There were times we all took chances, but they were all worth it. Watching you become the amazing adults you have become has been the best gift I could ever have been given.

There is no such thing as a perfect leader. Great leaders became great because they took a chance. Sometimes it worked and sometimes it didn't. But they took the chance. May you all take that chance in life and enjoy the journey!

Kathy Burrows

Table of Contents

Table of Contents

The First Potato Chip

LEADERSHIP STYLES

I have always loved to write. Even when very small, I kept a diary. As I got older, that diary evolved into journals of experiences I liked and experiences I didn't like and why. These journals became the cornerstone for me to review periodically as I started to lead, and I continue to now. Who did I have deep respect for? Who did I not want to emulate? Most importantly, why?

Going through my journals, I find negative leaders: the screamers, the "stay in your office and don't get involved" type, the "I keep a small group around me and we make all the decisions" type, the non-listeners, the "I want to be your best friend and want you to like me so I probably won't be helping you grow" type, and the "just do what I tell you to do" type.

Then I find the positive leaders: the listeners, the ones who say, "Here's something we need to focus on ... how do you all want to do this?" The ones who coach and help you grow. Those who praise in public and discuss problems in private. Those who don't let their bad day be your bad day. Those who realize they are only as good as the people around them, so they do everything in their power to grow their people to new heights.

Leadership starts early in life, and most often with our moms. Moms are amazing leaders as they motivate, coax, coach, build self-esteem, reprimand yet still believe in you, encourage you to take chances to grow, pick up the pieces if you fail, and brush you off and send you on your way again.

Moms know how to handle a budget, cut corners sensibly, know when to take that risk, and how to teach life's lessons. They never hide and are front and center every day of your developmental life. They are mentors forever. They manage an entire household and through strategic planning, get it all done. They have outstanding assessment skills as they know which friends of yours are true friends and which are not really your friends. They know YOU just as much as they know your siblings, what makes you different, what motivates you, what excites you, how you learn best, and what makes you tick. They teach us how to treat everyone equally and respectfully.

POTATO CHIP LEADERSHIP SKILLS

We start school and teachers become our leaders. Some work hard to make sure every student is given the best opportunity possible. They work individually after school so that everyone has the chance to succeed. They encourage, they impart knowledge, and they figure out what motivates us. Teachers realize there are different levels of learning within their four walls and that they can teach to all yet make sure those who are excelling are challenged and those who need that extra help are given it.

We start out in the work force and suddenly see a variety of leaders. There are those who invest in us and our growth and those who simply tell us what to do and hope we get it. The training wheels are off in life and we are thrown into a lot of life's valuable lessons.

One of the most insightful leaders I had the opportunity to meet while on my path to growth was Eric Nord, the founder of Nordson Corporation. He interviewed me for a scholarship when I was a senior in high school and planning to go to nursing school. This was the most challenging interview of my young life, as he asked me questions that had nothing to do with nursing but more about me as a person. To my surprise, I got the scholarship and we kept in touch until he passed away. I had sent him a letter when I left nursing and started sports, telling him I had hoped he was not disappointed in me.

Upon his death, his family sent me a letter that he had written to me and never mailed. He responded with the wisdom of a strong leader. Eric told me that everything we experience in life is to be viewed in multiple ways. My leadership training in nursing prepared me for a variety of futures, yet what he was most proud of was that I took that education and continued it, even if in a different role. He told me to "never be boxed in, but rather look for challenges that you can continue to share your strengths with." This is how I look at staff members now when I mentor. How can we share our strengths in different ways? How can we take our knowledge and use it in different ways? Instead of boxing in our staff, how can we open the doors and let them experience?

I still keep my journal going. I still see leaders who will never enable their staff to reach great heights. I also see leaders who continually challenge themselves to grow their staff. If you don't have a journal, it's time to start one. Who inspires you and why? Who do you not want to emulate and why? What styles have you seen that are positive and which have been negative? Most importantly, review those journals periodically. Are you representing the best of leadership styles?

THE FIRST POTATO CHIP

WHAT'S IN A NAME???

At least three times a week, I receive an email from someone who has been in the business for about 1 to 3 years and wants a title, whether it's Manager of Inside Sales, Manager of Ticket Sales, Manager of Premium, Director, and yes, some even feel they should be Vice President after a year. There is an obsession that equates success with titles.

News alert: Titles are a dime a dozen. We can create a title at a moment's notice, but does it mean anything? What makes us feel we need one quickly?

One of the most challenging areas I have found as a mentor is people wanting a title when they haven't even achieved success yet. How can you lead a sales team if you haven't hit your goal the past few years and proven yourself? How can you lead a sales team when you don't want to be a sales buddy to new hires and help them grow? Unfortunately, in sports sales we have put such an emphasis on call volume that I have had numerous sales reps tell me they deserve the next title because they consistently hit call volume. They haven't hit a sales goal, but they can call. What is the message we are sending to our staff to help them get ready for that next step, whatever it might be, in their career?

You've been in the business a year or 3 years and you don't want to sell anymore, you want to lead. There are a few steps to get where you want to go, and these include awareness of the job as well as steps to getting the job.

You will always sell, or at least you should. As a leader, you shouldn't have the largest sales goal, as your primary job is to coach your staff so they reach great heights and hit their goals. But you still need to sell. You still need to experience the ups and downs that they are experiencing. You still need to show that we all need to hit goals. You need to walk the walk and talk the talk. This is why I still sell and not just train. This is how we earn respect.

You should be doing the job before you get the job. You don't get a title and magically become a leader. You get the title because you are doing the job. This means that you are already stepping out of your comfort zone. You are hitting your sales goals, but you are also doing some leadership tasks. What can this be? Coaching a new hire. Mentoring someone struggling. Creating a motivating environment. Setting goals with the staff and challenging everyone, including yourself, to hit them. Practicing a sale a day. Encouraging power hours and leading them. Volunteering to recap the nightly report. Taking on new learning tasks, learning as much about the business as you can. Being a positive influence in the office. Creating a new sales strategy, but presenting it in a structured way, showing the benefits as well as any problems that may come from it and how you would overcome the problems. Going to your boss with a problem but having a potential solution that you suggest along with it. All these things prepare us for the title we want, whether in the organization we are in or one we are pursuing.

Rising from the ranks is the hardest leadership you will do. I've had many reps who have received the title they want and have attacked the new role as though they were President of the team. While this confidence is admirable, it doesn't give your staff much confidence. You don't have to have all the answers. Are your willing to put aside friendships and truly lead? Are you able to help them be the best they can be, whatever it takes, instead of being their best friend? There's a fine line between leading and friendship. It starts while you are a rep. Are you able to respect the people you work with but not be best buds? Do you complain to them about how things are being done, only to find as you move up that you don't want them complaining about you, so you really don't coach them to greatness but rather let them do as they want so they are happy? There's a lot of growth that comes with a title. Often it can be an empty feeling as the staff goes out to have beers and you are focusing on your strategy for the rest of the week. Can you draw that line? This is not to say you don't have fun with the staff. What it does say is that you hold yourself to a certain standard, both in your comments and your actions.

Hit your goals. I've had many reps who have asked me about wanting a title as manager of the department and when I ask how many years they've hit their goals they tell me they haven't yet. If you can't manage your own business, why would someone put you in a position to coach others to manage theirs? I've had reps who have not hit their goals, were put in a management position, and then stayed in that spot for 5+ years. They weren't ready for the next step as they hadn't proved themselves yet, and consequently struggled in their next role. Consequently, the sales team was never hitting their goal either. The goal of moving up is to continue moving up. The way we do that is by achieving goals.

Be part of the solution, not the problem. There will always be problems that come along. Are you one to complain about them or one to help fix them? Complaining breeds a negative culture. Finding ways to fix them breeds respect.

There's nothing wrong with wanting that next step. The key is, are you doing the steps to earn it? Or are you simply expecting it?

POTATO CHIP LEADERSHIP SKILLS

PROMOTION DOESN'T EQUAL SUCCESS

How often do you see the person who gets promoted is the top sales rep? One of the biggest mistakes we make in sports and business is simply promoting our best sales rep. Why is this a problem?

Promoting your best sales rep, especially when they are not ready for leadership and have been solely focused on numbers, sets them up to fail. Not having led, they now must focus on leadership, reports, strategies, and less time on selling. Their sales numbers slide, they are not sure how to help the team, and within 3 months you have a very frustrated leader. We give them no guidance and can't understand what their problem is as they were successful in selling. We give up on them. In essence, we have crushed their spirit.

If we believe someone has potential to be the leader, and they are our top seller, what can we do to help prepare them and see if they might be the right fit? What can we do overall to prepare our individual staff members for growth?

Give them select projects to work on. Observe how they handle a project as well as selling. Do they get frustrated? Do they find it exciting? Do they ask for help a lot or are they self-sufficient?

Have them mentor a new hire. Have them create a plan to coach the new hire for the first month. Observe how they coach. Do they seem upset to have to stop and answer questions or are they willing to help and encourage them? Is their strategy well thought out or simply a "make calls and close" type plan?

Ask them to create a new plan for one of the packages. How can it be sold differently, how should it be presented to staff, etc.? Are they able to step away from their focus on hitting personal goals to look at the bigger picture?

Ask them what they feel the quarterly focus should be. This can give you insight into if they are seeing the bigger picture or more focused on personal wins.

This is not to say a top sales rep should never be considered for a next level position; however, when we promote, it should be done with the intention of setting someone up for success. Are we doing that or hoping to hit numbers any way we can?

WHAT IS THE ULTIMATE GOAL?

I heard an old song by the Monkees (I know, you ask, "WHO???") on the radio the other day. It was "Pleasant Valley Sunday" and they were singing about "status symbol land." As I listened to the song, I thought of how we present what constitutes success to our staff and how it will either make or break them. Do we use titles as status symbols or use them sparingly? Do we reward in ways other than that coveted title, which becomes meaningless as many achieve it?

Titles were originally created to reward and lead. Little by little, they became a way to keep someone, earned or not. Our fear of losing someone led us to give away titles, which led to a lack of respect and a more chaotic culture. I remember one team whose president kept saying titles were not important, yet for everyone he brought aboard in a higher leadership role, he created an amazing title for them. This told the staff that, first of all, they were beyond top heavy with "leaders" and few workers, and also that this was a person you really couldn't trust. Is this the message we want to send?

What do we really need in titles and how can we reward in other ways? How should we be structuring our teams and when is too much too much?

I've had teams that have a President, a CEO, a CRO, two or three Executive Vice Presidents, two or four Senior Vice Presidents, six or seven Vice Presidents, Senior Directors, Directors, Senior Managers, Managers, Senior Account Reps, and by the way, some actual Account Reps who somehow seem to have to do the work of 50 people. Top heavy? I would say so.

What do we really need? Is the communication with all these people actually better or worse? In most instances, we find it's worse. Everyone seems to have their own tunnel focus and the organization suffers as a whole. Having a CEO and/or President depends on the size of the team and the scope of the business. Is the business one team or are there multiple properties? Having a CRO depends on if the focus is to utilize the facility for incremental revenue at other times throughout the year. Soccer teams, race tracks, and football fields seem to have the biggest need for CROs if they are looking to increase revenue. Do we really need Executive VPs, Sr. VPs and VPs? Again, are using increased titles to keep people? This is how we get top heavy.

When you focus on the job description of each person, you quickly realize that there is often a lot of crossover. Our goal should be to maximize communication by having a leader in each area that has multiple employees where the focus is specialized. For instance, if there are 15 employees in IT, it makes sense to have a

Director and a VP, just as in sales. If there are 5 employees in HR, is there really a need for a Sr. VP? Concessions are generally outsourced, so a VP in that area that also oversees Merchandise might be a smarter move.

The point is, don't have so many leaders that you have few workers to actually do the most important jobs … creating revenue.

This leads us to how can we reward in other ways? How can we keep our organizations from being top heavy with titles to a more spirited, ownership approach to the business by the employees without giving them all another name? More often than not, specialty projects or niche markets with them creating the strategy for it and the sales approach is a winner for many reps. Knowing they have an opportunity to grow a portion of the business, work with the VP on it, present it to everyone and then fulfill the plan gives one a sense of accomplishment. A bonus upon completion for a job well done always works well and goes hand in hand.

What does this do? This enables the reps to grow in different ways. They are learning leadership skills: planning, building, executing, presenting, and fulfilling. They now have invested in the organization and have done far more to bring in revenue than many with titles that are in meetings most of the day. These are the people you reward with a bonus for a job well done.

On the flip side, I encourage reps to not be afraid to take on more and offer ideas. A VP I once worked with started as an intern, became a sales rep, and always offered to do whatever needed to be done. If he didn't know how to do it, he researched and learned so he could be an asset. He wasn't concerned with titles but rather with learning and growing. He wanted all the tools he could possibly learn before he started moving. That work ethic and focus over the course of time helped him rise to an Executive VP.

I just met with a rep who had the opportunity to move up with a title, but in essence doing the same job, or taking another job that many would consider a lateral move but enabled him to grow considerably. He chose the growth opportunity. In the long run, his career will flourish by all he is learning, the projects he will be working on, and the ideas he will be able to cultivate. This is a rep who has invested in his career.

Most sales reps want to feel valued. A title is great but given a project and the freedom to develop it from start to finish, recognition in front of your peers for a job well done, and a bonus goes a long way to a person feeling vested in the organization. The title will come when the opportunity is there. Creating many titles dilutes their purpose and loses the respect of the staff.

ARE YOU READY TO MOVE UP?

Promotions. Everyone wants to be a leader. Everyone's goal is to be a manager or director. That day comes. And then?

How often have you seen someone get promoted and start their new position with no guidance, no background, and no support system? They are to function as their predecessor and their predecessors before them. Fit the mold. Don't make waves. Make sure you manage by numbers. And what happens? Sports get stuck in the routine it is now. Departments don't grow. There's a lot of turnover. No creativity. No true leadership. Not developing and coaching the up and coming generation that will soon be leading sports. You have a department once again that is measured by numbers (generally call volume and meetings set) instead of a department managed by development.

What should a promotion to a leadership role look like? Look at leadership candidates, not who sold the most.

Ownership of position. You are not your predecessor. Chances are you sell a little differently than those around you. You may want more training, more understanding. Do I want to manage? Or do I want to coach? Do I want to manage by numbers or manage what I can control, thus developing each and every individual under me? You should be free to set up new systems, truly develop your people and open the floor to staff input and strategy.

A leader above them who wants to continue to develop them. Once promoted, it should not be an island. There should be trust, coaching, and lots of listening on the new leader's supervisor's part. We simply can't announce their promotion then expect them to jump in and be at 100% right away, no matter how long they've worked there.

Continuing education. Just because you got promoted, the learning shouldn't stop. And not just learning about sales. Learning about how people learn, what motivates them, how to build trust, etc.

POTATO CHIP LEADERSHIP SKILLS

An understanding of their role. The new leader should be a coach for his or her team. Sales trainers should not be brought in year after year for basic training principles and role playing. That is for those new in sales and that's where you come in as a leader. Your coaching should be a continual reminder of basic sales and role playing should be a part of the culture. Coaching 1:1 weekly with measurable techniques to get better is key. Trainers who take that staff to the next level are what should be utilized for their growth. The leader then should make sure that that next level is built into the culture so the team can continue to achieve on a broader scale.

What should a good leadership training look like?

- Teams that really want to develop their people should invest in them. So what does a leadership training look like?

- structuring your week vs putting out fires; coaching to strengths

- building your team: getting to know your staff, building fun and shared occasions, developing values

- evaluations: ongoing vs yearly; how to motivate in an evaluation

- interviewing: managing the interview to find the right person to fit the culture/change the culture vs a warm body to sell

- coaching through accountability: how it leads to performance improvement

- letting go: delegating and providing ownership to enable the staff to become part of the process rather than a person who provides numbers/revenue; letting go of sales meetings, morning huddle and empowering your people

- creating your coaching plan: what does a 1:1 coaching session look like? Knowing how each team member learns

- utilizing brainstorming sessions: using the brain or creating a storm?

- managing up

- writing department strategies. Coaching your team in developing personal quarter strategies

- be a change mentor

- creating and utilizing a strong onboarding process

- how to motivate and inspire

- creating great culture

- handling a problem employee before it infects the staff

- knowing how each of your people learn and focusing on that in your 1:1s

- creating the next leader

It's most exciting when you announce promotions. Aspirations are being achieved, perceived opportunities to change things get us excited, and then …

Make sure that with your promotions comes an investment. Investing in your people, be it the sales reps or the leaders, is our job as an executive leadership team. Our goal in promoting is to enable that new leader to build their own culture, create their own department, and make the changes they feel are best for the team. The way to do that is through education, understanding what leadership truly is, mentoring, and empowering.

POTATO CHIP LEADERSHIP SKILLS

EVERY TEAM HAS A COACH

Look at a baseball team. They have the coach, the bench coach, first-base coach, third-base coach, pitching coach, hitting coach, infield coach, outfield coach and more. Basketball has head coaches, assistant coaches, and more. Just think of all the coaches a sports team has. And they call them all "coaches." They just assign them a specialty.

Why do we feel the need to create a hierarchy structure that many want but so few can attain? Why don't we structure our sales teams in much the same way?

What if, instead of the limited career path of Manager/Director/VP/President or GM, we actually create in the office what our sports teams are really like on the field, the court, the ice, the pitch, etc.? What if we grew people by levels, just like many businesses do with Level 1, Level 2, Level 3, etc, but use the sports analogy?

For example, what if we had our Head Coach and Assistant Head Coach, and moved our sales reps through varying degrees of coaching based on their growth? Initially they are all Bench Coaches. But then they grow to be Season Coach, Business Development Coach, Area Sales Scouts (having a market of their own to pursue based on location or areas of categories), Regional Sales Scouts (oversee a region of sales such as northeast regional sales scout, focusing on all businesses northeast of the team within a three-hour radius), General Manager of Sales, which gives the rep the ability to use their creativity and ideas to bring aboard new business, test new ways of operating, and grow and show best practices for all the sales reps they work with. It's a position one in sales would aspire to.

It used to be that sales in sports was the steppingstone to any position. It's not that way anymore. Leaders want to develop true salespeople and grow them. But when they do, they fail to promote them for the craft they are so good at. What if, as leaders, we started to view this, not as a typical sports promotion, but truly as a smart business career promotion.

After all, sales IS and should be a true career. Not just a position we have with only one way to grow. Career growth. I challenge all sports teams to start looking at their sales reps as the true Sales Professionals they are, create a true sports culture along with naming levels, and not be afraid to grow their career in sales and move them forward. Let's get our teams moving into the future instead of stuck in the past!

Potato Chip Trainers

Create a journal of leadership styles.

- Identify patterns as to what motivates you in styles and what demotivates you.

- If you were in that role, how would you handle it?

- What might be the expected outcome? Who leads well in these areas? What do they do differently to make it successful?

Make a list of what you can be doing to prepare for the title you want.

- What areas do you find you need to grow in?

- How can you prepare yourself to grow in these areas? Create a plan.

- What can you do in this growth role to help the organization now?

Define projects for reps that could be a step to growth.

- Ask yourself: what area will this help them grow in? Clearly define the expectations.

- Let them create the plan and the strategy, build the plan, and then present it to management. Once approved, let them execute.

- Enable them to present the results to the entire team. Recognize their efforts. Bonus if a job well done.

Create simple leadership strategies for everyone to feel engaged at some point.

- Team up new hires with a sales buddy. Have them define how they will help them through the first 3 months. Have them set goals with the new hire—motivating, inspiring, and educating them.

- Have them present a 15-minute sales workshop at a sales meeting. Give them the chance to educate and grow their peers.

- Let them have ownership of sales meetings. Eighty percent of talking should be done by them, not you as the leader. If you are doing 80%, I can promise they are not listening.

Create a promotion strategy by week.

- Focus on a different way to invest in their training and growth each week.

- Create the how and the plan to execute.

- Create a plan to grow your sales staff using sports terminology for a structured career path.

The Second
Potato Chip

AVOIDING HAVING A MINI-ME

You're putting your leadership team together. You interview. You step back when someone comes up with ideas different from yours and fear they may "rock the boat." When putting your leadership team together, do you tend to look at those who:

- Have the same concepts as you?

- The same thought process?

- The same ideas?

- Have the most in common with everyone else on the leadership team and will be most easily accepted?

- Will keep the sales staff in the same structure as they've always been?

- Do you find yourself thinking that it is "easier" to manage and work with someone who is, in essence, just like you?

Leaders who hire "mini-me's" (people just like or similar to themselves) will find in a short time that they have done a great disservice to their teams, departments, and organization. This group will grow to lack creativity, energy, challenging of ideas, and stimulation. As a leader, we all need to get out of our comfort zone and bring together a more diverse leadership team.

Diversity isn't just about race, gender, age, or ethnic group. It is also about how people perceive ideas, the varying strengths they have (which hopefully are not the same as yours), and how they interact with others. A diverse environment will bring the four quadrants of Strengthfinders to success: Executing, Influencing, Relationship Building, and Strategy. It enables us all to leave the "because that's the way we do it" mentality and open our minds to endless possibilities. It challenges us to think in ways out of our comfort zone. It enables our staff to become energized, creative, stimulated, and harmonious if done well. And it leads to trust, hope, and team engagement.

POTATO CHIP LEADERSHIP SKILLS

Before you assign your next leader for your team, sit down and review ALL the staff you currently have. Look at them through "evaluating" eyes:

- Are there any who are:

- Stellar communicators?

- Great at influencing?

- Able to promote harmony by accepting diverse ideas?

- Willing to dig in and go after the job at hand without a lot of explaining, no matter how different the job is?

- Of an analytical mind?

- Good strategists?

- Repairers of damaged relationships?

- Able to maximize a situation?

- Flexible and able to switch to a plan B or C?

- Quick thinking?

- Deliberative and think through a decision?

- Great at getting people on "their bus"?

- Great coaches?

Remember one key thing: **you, as a leader, are only as good as the people around you**. You don't have to have all the ideas and all the answers; but you do need a team that can bring those ideas and answers to the table. Build your leadership team with varying strengths, not mini-me's. If you find your leadership team always in agreement, look for someone who is more deliberative. If you and your leadership team get sidetracked easily, look for someone with focus who will keep the project moving. If you and your leadership team like to "try ideas out of the blue," look for someone who is analytical to help think it through. If you and your leadership team control a meeting, look for someone who is individualistic who can draw out everyone's thoughts.

Evaluating your people for their strengths, versus who is most similar to everyone else, can bring together a leadership team that will benefit the entire organization, challenge the status quo, and stimulate great thinking. As a leader, you will look brilliant. As members of the leadership team, your people will grow, and you'll have great leadership via a diverse group of people. The only "mini-me" you should want shared is offering the best you have, while learning from them and the best they have to offer!

POTATO CHIP LEADERSHIP SKILLS

RISING UP THRU THE RANKS

You've done it! You got promoted! You are now the Manager or Director of the team you've been working at for a few years. This is going to be exciting. Since you already know everyone, this should be a piece of cake. Right?

Rising from within is sometimes the hardest promotion you will ever have. That line is drawn between hanging out for a beer after work, talking or complaining about things, to now setting strategy and coaching. What are some of the changes you need to make in order to have the staff respect you in your new role while embracing the changes that come with it?

Water cooler conversations stop. Remember, you were in their shoes. You had conversations where you vented about leadership, decisions, other coworkers, etc. Now is the time to excuse yourself from these. Occasional after-hours beers or lunches with the team are great, but continually being part of the group does not give your staff the ability to help distinguish your new role. Your role is to be friendly without being friends.

Communicate your goal clearly. Now that you are in this leadership role, let the team know that your #1 mission is to help coach them all to success. You are there for them to grow and continue to develop. You are keeping the seat warm for the next person to rise. Let them know you will have their back and will help them work through any problems they have. This helps the communication changes that are needed from the start.

Meet with each team member one on one. Let them know your vision but more importantly, ask them for input in this vision. How can 'we' make these changes together? How can 'we' help our team get to new heights? Incorporating their input says, "I may be the leader, but I am also bringing you along with me, not setting out ahead of you, expecting you to follow on your own. We are in this together."

Communicate. This is the one thing most teammates complain about when a peer gets promoted. The leader suddenly goes silent. If you want your team to succeed, open communication is necessary. If you can change something that is needed, that is great. If you can't, explain why. Use what you learned from the 1:1s to discuss with the whole team. Plan your strategy together. This "we" mentality gives the team the opportunity to buy in to the vision you have in mind. Communicate what ideas are working. Those that are not, ask for suggestions on how to make them work better. Let them be part of the process.

Earn their respect. You do this by what you do each and every day. Do you sit five feet from them yet send an email every time instead of communicating verbally? Do you sit down and have power hours with them, knowing you also have a goal? Do you see that they may have a lot on their plate and pull them together and help prioritize what is most important and how it can be achieved?

Acknowledge their role in your successes. I had someone reach out to me who shared that they brought in a great sponsorship, yet the Director took all the credit. Acknowledging your teams' contributions in the department's success is key to earning respect and creating a true culture of teamwork. Taking credit for things others have a role in without acknowledging them breeds distrust, disrespect, and breaks down culture.

Empower. One of the worst things we can do as we move up is have a "take charge" attitude in which we issue our expectations without letting the team have a role in it. Letting them take charge of certain projects and giving them the opportunity to run with them shows your trust in them and earns your respect.

Get the title out of your head and focus on how you can best help your team. Think about all the times you led a work project. It was important to have everyone contribute, but the results were not always going the way you hoped. At that point, you had to work with the individual areas where the project wasn't on task and figure out how to make it work. It's much the same now. Empower them. Help them. Be there for them if they need help. This is not to say you are doing their job, but your focus is to help grow your team.

You are only as good as they are. Your focus now shifts to how you can best help each individual grow. Remember, you can't manage numbers but you can coach people to help their hit numbers and that's how you hit a goal. If you're not helping them succeed, you are going to have to hit a goal yourself. That's not leading. That's not recognizing your role as coach.

Grow your self-confidence. If you are unsure, your team will feed off of that. Anxiety sets in and the team feels paralyzed. If you are confident and display that confidence, if you display confidence in them, they will feed off of this and take more ownership in their business.

This is an exciting time. Embrace your new role. Think before you speak. Teammates often view leadership as going over to "the dark side." It doesn't have to be this way. All you simply have to do is establish a vision, invite your team to be part of the vision, and ask how they can best help get to where you are all going, and then let them take active roles. When you invite your team to be part of the process instead of simply a means to the end, you invite energy. Energy is what creates great culture in your group. And creating great culture is something every leader hopes to achieve.

BULL OR COMFY CAT MANAGEMENT

A leadership role with a new team is a whole new opportunity to share ideas, create change, and make our mark. All too often we go in doing one of two things: try to win everyone over right away, hope to be everyone's friend, or going in and making loads of changes within the first 60 days.

What happens to the team in these instances? They take a step back, dig in their heels and reject all this cheery change and friendship mentality or find themselves in total chaos with all the changes. What is wrong?

Moving in to a new leadership role doesn't mean we have to overturn a whole department in 30 days. A smart new leader will take time to get to know the staff, meet with them, listen, assess, assess some more, make simple starting suggestions, and most importantly give the team a chance to have a voice. A smart new leader will let the process that is in place continue until trust is earned and then work with the team to make changes that can grow their team.

I once knew a leader who was a bit overly excited to come into their new role, and within 2 weeks had the entire staff quit. Why? Day one he told them that he had great ideas to change things so they could get good ... which implied they weren't good. Day two he told them they were all making calls wrong and handed out sheets of how he wanted the calls to go ... which told them the success they were already having was wrong. Day three he told them they had to make 60 calls before they could go to lunch and another 60 before they could go home ... thereby managing numbers instead of focusing on coaching for results. The list goes on. His superior let this go on week one and week two—by Thursday of week two, half the staff quit, and on Friday the rest quit. Could this have been avoided? Absolutely. Should his superior have been coaching him? One would think. Unfortunately, he was also out a month later.

Let's look at how we can best take on this new role with a new team:

Introductions. Spend an hour or so with your new team introducing yourself and your background and then going around the room having each introduce themselves and their background. Ask them questions. Show interest. Comment on things they've learned in the industry and ask each who has been the biggest inspiration to their growth and why.

POTATO CHIP LEADERSHIP SKILLS

Have borderless walls. Don't barricade yourself up into an office and not step out. Sure you will have a lot to learn and a lot on your plate. Respect is earned. If you have an office, spend an hour or two each day working on whatever it is you are learning while sitting with the team. Listen to the culture. Listen to the conversations. Interject a comment upon hearing a job well done. The best way to get to know your team is by being among them throughout the day, not away from them.

Set up one on ones. Get to know each person. Ask them about them … 80% of the talking should be by them. How do they best learn? (This is key to your coaching.) What do they enjoy most about their sales role? What do they find most tedious about their sales role? What do they think could bring in more sales if changed? What do they like to do in their off time? What has this job taught them so far? How do they plan their day? How do they structure an idea?

Assess and keep assessing. Listen to conversations on the phone. Are there conversations where they are building a relationship or is it "buy, buy, buy" or "Hi … I'd like to set up a meeting to discuss how my product can help you" mentality? Where do you feel the most help can be given in that area? Listen to how they describe the options available. How well do they know the product? How happy and passionate are they about the product? Do they feel what they are offering is really valuable or just what they were told to sell? How do they interact with others? What is the daily culture like? How do they start their day—as islands or as a team with a huddle? What is their daily structure? Do they have a strategy plan? Do they know where the company is going and what their role is in that journey? Do they have a voice or have they simply been told to be callers?

Make only minor suggestions after the first couple of weeks. Gradually work your way into offering suggestions. Make the suggestions during your 1:1s to give your team members something measurable to work on when they leave a coaching session instead of simply asking what is in their pipeline. Giving them something measurable to improve on sends the message that you care about their well-being and growth.

Host a team meeting after the first 30 days to share. This is when you start to share a vision. The first meeting is sharing some of the assessments you've made: what the team feels is working or not. Write it down on a whiteboard. Ask them their thoughts on how we could make what's working even better and what changes they feel need to be made for what is not. How would they make these changes? This starts to engage them in being part of the process.

Host your next team meeting with the intention of starting to create change. Knowing what your vision is, and knowing what some of the problems are, now you ask for input in making changes. Which two things during the next quarter should be the biggest focus? How can we best focus on it? What would be the steps to success? What would everybody's role be? How would we measure success? Before everyone leaves the meeting, have a strategy and plan in place for the next 3 months. Make it measurable. Appoint a team leader for the quarter who will help make the growth fun. Announce the celebration that will be held at the end of the quarter when the focus is achieved. Let them know they are working toward something.

Be part of the process yourself. If they are focusing on increasing premium sales, then make some of the calls yourself. If they create a plan, ask what they want your role to be.

Be the quiet, strong leader. You don't have to be the only one heard to lead. If you care about creating the right energy and culture, 80% of conversation and ideas will be coming from them. Let them lead meetings. Let them lead huddles. You are there as a guide.

Patience is a virtue we often have to learn. Patience in a new role that you have come to in a new place is key to success. We are often asked to be change agents. We have to remember that a change agent is not synonymous with being a charging bull, stumbling around, stamping our feet wanting to be heard, seen, followed and feared. A change agent is more that of a cat in a comfortable house that walks around assessing, listening, observing … and occasionally makes itself heard and his wants noted.

EARNING LOYALTY & RESPECT

Do you wish your staff had passion and loyalty to you and your organization? How do you get to be a leader who has such deep respect and loyalty? Stepping in to the position is not the easiest thing in the world. If the former boss was highly respected and liked, it takes time. If the former boss was not really well liked, there is caution. Either way, respect and loyalty are earned.

How?

Being a true Leader means …

The office is not four walls but rather an organization.

A company is built with people not titles. Know more about your team than just the Executive Floor. Walk around and see the people who make your company happen on a daily basis. See what their job entails. Understand the number of hours and work they put in. Comment to them about a job well done or an extraordinary amount of effort they are putting into a project.

Get to know your people.

We should never know them as the revenue they bring in or the systems they keep running. Know their name, a little about them, acknowledge them by name and show you care when things happen to them or their family members. I was privileged to know a well-known CEO of a global company and was impressed with the loyalty and deep respect the staff had for him. His staff told me that no matter the number of employees or departments he would go to, he learned about everyone, from executives to cleaning staff, and he had something relevant about them to say to each. He showed he cared about them as people, not as workers, and for that, they said they would run through walls for him.

Care about the development of your people.

Not everyone wants to do today's job forever. Most of us want to reach for more stars. Know about this, encourage their growth, and encourage your executive team to be an active participant in that growth. Bring people in specifically to work with them on their development and show it is just as important to you as to them.

Don't just talk the talk. Walk the walk.

Company-speak often gets lost. The message is loud and clear when all employees see their leader actively living it every day. Be the inspiration and your staff will follow. As leaders we should delegate. But sometimes, when staff is overwhelmed, we can delegate to ourselves. This makes a huge statement.

Insulation is for houses: Don't put up insulation with your "inner team."

Your team is your company, your organization, not just your decision makers. Take part in department meetings, from custodial to executive. Ask questions, learn. Show you really do care about every facet of the organization.

Thank your team. Your success depends on them.

Walking around, stopping to talk, and thanking your people does more for the heart than any gift. It shows your employee that they are more to you than the person that was hired for that seat. *It gives that employee that inner smile that comes from being appreciated ... priceless.* I go back to encouraging all leaders and all newcomers to an organization to keep a journal of leadership styles ... things you like, don't like. The positive impact, the negative. And as you start your climb up that ladder, pull that journal out occasionally so you don't become that isolated individual that you dreaded as you were in your early stages.

Living the golden rule really is the secret!

GREAT SALES CULTURE MISSION STATEMENTS

When I work with a team, I ask if they have a Mission Statement, and if they do, what is it? Answers range from "No," to "Yes," to "I don't really know." Rarely can anyone tell me their mission statement if they do have it. Why is this? Generally, the company mission statement was made by someone other than them, so their thumbprint is not on it. It's glossed over when hiring and never used on a day-to-day basis.

You can have 50 people on your sports sales team, and you can have 50 islands working independently, not having a clue of their teammate's successes, challenges, or questions. Or you can have 50 people on your sports sales team that are working as a team, sometimes in pairs, with strengths, and ultimately all working together and challenging each other to achieve success. You know what you have on the field, court, or ice. Do you know what you have in the office?

Great culture starts when everyone buys in. But how to get them to that point? **Your mission statement and values.**

If your team has a mission statement, who created it? Was it input from an exec group? A committee? Was the team asked for input? If the team has a mission statement, more importantly, *does your department?* Think about it … a mission statement should be a living, breathing statement of what your organization stands for. But in order to get to that point, every department has to feed into that overall statement. Does yours?

An organizational mission statement is key but is worth very little if each department does not have their own statement that lives the organizational one. And how do you do that? By asking your sales team, marketing team, communications team, service team, all departments, to create their own that feeds into the overall organization statement. This is the single most important meeting your sales team (or whatever department) will have: the opportunity to put into words what it is they stand for and their values.

During your off season, your sales department should have a focus day: where they were last year, what is the goal for this year, what worked, what didn't, ideas to make experiences better, how to best use their individual strengths, ideas to change sales and then … what is it we stand for? What are the values needed to do this? Brainstorming for this is crucial. Everyone's input is important. Ideas are jotted down. A sales department mission statement is created and values are listed. What the values mean *to them* is listed. The key is it has to come from the sales team, not an exec team and not a committee. *This is the story of them … who they are, why they work there, why they do the job they do, how it is they want to connect with their clients. There is no more important statement than this.*

Once created and agreed upon, this should be on their desk in front of them as well as in front of you as their leader each and every day. This is our commitment, our reason for getting up each day and doing what we do. This is what you live up to. This is our promise. What happens then? You have a team who is focused *together*, all working for a common goal. There is accountability. There is a spirit of oneness. There is a team.

While with the El Paso Chihuahuas this year, we discussed the department mission statement. While on a team retreat, Sr. Director Nick Seckerson helped lead his sales staff to define who they are and why they came to work each day ... why they do what they do. This is what they created:

Mission Statement: "We believe in being problem-solvers for the El Paso community. We strive to provide the highest and best atmosphere, platform and support system to every El Paso family, business, and organization in order to create unforgettable memories and experiences for all.

Core Values:

- *Have passion: create it, exude it, share it.*

- *Take pride: follow through on our words and our commitments.*

- *Engage: provide exceptional service to guests, the community, and teammates at all times.*

- *Get in the game: contribute, challenge, collaborate, grow.*

- *Leave no doubt: exceed expectations."*

I don't think I've seen a mission statement and values as strong as this ... in reading it, can you not see each staff member, each belief, each commitment? This sums up who the El Paso Chihuahuas' sales staff is and why they are doing their job. This not only tells me their commitment to the community but also to each other. This tells me why giving their all each and every day makes for success. This is what great leadership does, from the ownership to the President, GM, Sr. Director, Managers, and each rep.

Do you keep it forever? No. Sales teams change, sales change, beliefs change. Every couple of years this should be revisited. Does it still hold? Should something be added/deleted? What can we do differently to be successful?

Successful teams, such as El Paso, have less turnover, more commitment, more growth, and a stronger relationship with their community because they believe, as a department, and ultimately as an organization, in why they are there.

If your team is in the off season, and you don't have the same buy-in, it's time to stop, breathe, and realize why it is you are there. Create your sales team mission statement. List the values you must have and what they mean. Live it. Breathe it. It can and will change the entire culture.

MANAGING UP

Everyone thinks that coming up through the ranks can be a challenge. Some feel that coming from outside to a new organization can be a big challenge. In reality, one of the biggest challenges you will ever face is managing up.

How often have we felt intimidated by our supervisor? Walking in, never knowing for sure how they will react to what we have to share. Presenting our plan and not knowing if they will be happy, offer constructive criticism, or be sarcastic toward us. So many of our biggest nightmares in leadership is not from the team we work with but rather the team we work for.

The key to managing up is managing that fine balancing act. To do this, you need to know where your leaders are in the process in relationship to where you as a leader are in the process. Do you balance each other? Are you polar opposites? Are there similarities but definite differences?

What are the steps to Managing Up?

Communication. Communication is—or at least should be—a two-way street. Top down communication is open dialogue, understanding, and a happier staff. How do you do this with your leader?

Listen. The hardest thing for us to do is listen intently. We hear, but do we really listen. I've been guilty so many times of having the thought process totally understood in my head, only to have it come out of my mouth in a different way. It's what the leader says and doesn't say that is important. Take notes. Don't rely on your brain to remember it all.

Adapt. What is your leader's communication style? Don't make them change for you. Instead adapt to their style as best you can.

Two-way Communication. You, as a leader, report to your boss. They, as a leader, report to their boss. The worst thing that can happen is for your leader to be caught off guard and vice versa. Two-way communication will make it more comfortable for both of you as leaders.

Ask questions. If you are not sure of what your leader is telling you, ask. Make sure that the communication is very clear so that you leave the meeting knowing exactly what your next steps are.

Confirm. Make sure before you leave the room you have confirmed next steps.

Get feedback. If you're not having coaching sessions, ask for them. Getting feedback is essential to working together smoothly.

The best surprise is no surprise.

Report in regularly. If you do, you alleviate the unknown for your boss.

Address potential and existing problems. Trying to hide them definitely won't endear you. The key: when you bring the problem, bring a potential solution or two. Without a potential solution, you are simply asking your boss to do your job.

Know your boss's agenda.

What's on their plate? Oftentimes, they may have a lot going on and your question about an upcoming contest you want to have is not the most important thing in the world right now. Know what's on their plate. Know what's keeping them up at night. In what way can you assist?

Prioritize. Know your boss's priorities at the time. This will help you focus your team on what is most important for the organization as a whole.

Get in synch. If they are focusing on 2 months left and 40% to goal, then that is your focus.

Be proactive. Knowing your boss's agenda will help you be proactive. It will enable you to create better recap charts so as to answer the questions he might be asking. It will enable you to refocus your team so that you are already working on what he will need you to focus on. Get in sync with your boss's style.

Reports. How do they want reports? Nightly? Weekly? How detailed? What will they most want to know? Anticipate so they don't have to ask you. More is better than less.

Format. What is their ideal format to receive information? Are they chart driven? Stats driven? Bullet point? Excel? Do they want once a day reporting or once a week?

Communication. What is their preferred method of communication? Email? In person? Daily recap? Bullet points?

Meetings. What are their expectations in meetings? Are you prepared? Are you proactive or fumbling?

Early/late. Is your boss early in or late out? When are they freshest and you find you can communicate with them best. That is when you should be there.

Know your boss's hot buttons.

Tardiness. It's important for you as a leader to not be late but emphasize being on time with your team. How you react and how you encourage your team to act speaks volumes for you as a leader.

Speech. Do they appreciate slang? Do they tolerate occasional swearing? Do they never use it? Emulate how they speak.

Noise. Do they tolerate a more chaotic atmosphere or a more focused atmosphere? Create it.

When to go over your boss's head.

Rare instances. This would have to be an HR situation.

Document and be quiet. Documenting is key and not discussing with your team is essential.

Strengths and weaknesses.

List your boss's strengths and weaknesses:

List your strengths and weaknesses:

Compensating. Where do they need your support? How can you best help where they are weak and they best grow you where you are?

The goal to success is managing up is to make life easier for them. Anticipate, support, be a right arm. These are the qualities that will let your leader have time then to take you on the journey versus letting you sink or swim on your own.

Potato Chip Trainers

Look at your current leadership team:

- Who challenges you?

- Who is most like you?

- Who is more of a "yes" person?

- Who is quick to offer suggestions with/without a valid reason?

- Who is more deliberative in their decisions?

- Who has the most respect from their team?

- Who yields the best results from their team? Why?

Now ask yourself: is my team balanced? Does it weigh more to one side? What areas could we improve on for balance? This is who I should look for in my next leadership promotion.

I just came up through the ranks of my team. What is my strategy for success?

Create a checklist of ways to bring my team along with me.

- Identify the vision for the team.

- Set up 1:1 coaching sessions weekly or biweekly.

- Plan my strategy for each prior to the session.

- What one new thing can I learn about them?

- What one or two things that are measurable can I give them to work on for the next week or two to help them get to that next level.

- Acknowledge great work.

- Review nightly and make sure you acknowledge when someone has done something great, brought in a big sale, went above and beyond in making things happen.

- Who else can you enlist in leadership to recognize great moments? What will be the plan?

Look at projects coming up.

- Which can you turn over to certain staff members and empower them to take ownership of?

- **I'm a new leader with a new team.** What is my strategy for success?

- Each time I want to jump in to change something, write it down instead.

- Keep a "change journal." Exercise patience.

- Read it 2 weeks later. Is this still a change worth making or not?

Fine tune your assessment skills.

- Sit in with your team during power hours. Listen to one person each power hour. What would set them up for success?

- Make notes for coaching of things that are being communicated well, and things that are not.

- **First two months:** If you want to introduce some suggestions, make no more than two suggestions of minor changes after thinking on them.

- Ask the team how we can facilitate them.

Create your strategy for your 30-day meeting.

- What is your vision for the department?

- Ask the team to think about the how this can be done for the next meeting.

- Host your second meeting and listen to ideas.

- Brainstorm ideas.

- Ask the team which they feel will best work for the upcoming quarter.

- Have them create the "how."

- List ways you can be part of the process.

- Be involved and let them know you are on the journey with them.

- Earning respect.

- Practice MBWA … management by walking around. Don't sit in your office all day.

- Make a list of what you know about each rep.

- Write down where each rep wants to be next.

Create ideas of how you can help get them there.

- Show appreciation. Before you leave each night, is there someone who has gone above and beyond? Did they hit a hard goal?

- After hours, send an email, leave a post-it, or leave a voicemail expressing your appreciation. Let that be the first acknowledgement they get the next morning to set their day up for success.

Start to create a positive culture.

- With staff, create a department mission statement or update the current one.

- Read the organizational mission statement. Ask what this means to the team.

- Ask for ways we can fulfill the organizational statement in our own ticket sales department. List them.

- Have the staff develop no more than 4 sentences from the list that creates their statement.

POTATO CHIP LEADERSHIP SKILLS

Know your boss. Manage up.

- List your boss's strengths and weaknesses. List yours. Make a list of areas you can best support them.

- List your boss's communication style. Plan your days to communicate in the style most effective. If they want reports at 5pm, give them to them at 4pm.

- Anticipate your boss's needs for the upcoming week based on what is on his plate. What can you have ready or at least started before being asked?

The Third
Potato Chip

GROWING LEADERS

We promote or bring in a new Sales Manager, or Director, or even VP. We put them in their role. And then we wait and see what they do. After all, they are in the role, so they should know what they are doing and lead now, right? If they hit the goal, then they must be outstanding and we look brilliant for bringing them in.

Meanwhile, our newly promoted leader feels one of two ways: either that they are pretty good or they are stressed and unsure. They want to believe our team thinks that they are doing a great job, and they focus on making sure the department hits their numbers goal. If they do, then they must be a *great* leader.

If stressed and unsure, we find they can't make a decision. They hesitate every step of the way. The staff feeds off of this and anxiety in the department sets in. Goals are not hit or are sporadic. Our leader doesn't know which way to turn and finds themselves digging a deeper hole.

The question is, have you set them up for success or failure from day one? Leadership is not a role that you wind up and let run. It takes earning respect, training, development, 1:1s, and solid planning. I have often found teams that manage their new leaders on a happy note the first three months and through intimidation thereafter. This only starts a chain reaction, as this is often how they will start managing their sales team. Soon, everyone is miserable.

How can we, as management, help our new young leaders on the path to success?

Here are some thoughts, and I encourage you to comment and share yours:

Training doesn't stop when someone is in a management position. One of the biggest pitfalls I've seen has been a lack of training or a "one stop shop" for management 101. Management isn't learned in one class. It isn't learned just by trying things out. It's learned through education and understanding. How do my individual staff members learn? How can I communicate best to get my message across in general and to each individual? How can I recognize and then best use their strengths? How can I learn to manage up? How do I learn to manage across? How do I come across confident without coming across arrogant? How can I show I'm willing to listen when my supervisors are clamoring at me to get results ASAP? Is anyone going to help me or do I have to sit and read this book and learn on my own? Is anyone going to invest in me?

Coach them by teaching them how to let go ... and do it yourself. A micromanaging exec will bring angst to the leader, which in turn will bring pressure to the sales team. Show you trust them. Let them use their mind and, most importantly, encourage them to let their staff use theirs.

Provide coaching moments. Coach your young protégé on action/reaction. Coach them through some of the issues they are facing and how actions will cause different reactions. This is a great opportunity for them to learn from you.

Provide timely answers. If you provide timely answers, it encourages them to give timely answers to their staff. If you do not, you set them up from the start to lose respect from their staff. You are part of the equation.

Evaluating your Managers/Directors. Do you wait for the yearly or twice-yearly request sent out by HR or are you truly investing in their growth? If an evaluation is done once or twice a year, you are throwing things at people they may not have realized were issues. Everyone should have biweekly 1:1s and evaluations every 3 months. With 1:1s, each person should be given something concrete to work on as a leadership tool for the next couple of weeks. In the 3-month evaluations, a larger leadership project should be given for them to focus on during the next 3 months. This keeps the investment growing and gives them the opportunity to continue learning.

Your role should be trusted Coach/Mentor, not best buddy. Our young sales leaders are looking for someone they can learn from and respect. They don't need a best buddy in this role. Be that coach or mentor and you will find someone who works harder, wants to succeed, and will treat their staff in the same way. This positive learning tool helps show them how to lead their own staff.

Talk the talk and walk the walk. Want them to sell more? Sell the product yourself. Want them to set better goals? Show he/she how you have arrived at the goals you set for them. Want them to communicate better? Make sure your communication is up to par and clear and concise. Lead them through examples. As the exec, we need to be the example of what they want to strive to be.

Put money in the budget for outside experiences. It is beyond me how sales leaders want to grow, attend conferences and meetings that will enhance their thinking, grow their team and organization, and yet we tell them they have to pay for it themselves. Every budget needs to have education and conferences outside their walls built into it for an opportunity each year or every other year. Why are we so behind in sports and entertainment? Because we keep doing the same things, year after year, or use what other teams are doing without going outside the confines of our league to meet and learn from others in the industry and challenging ourselves and our minds. Let your leader grow. Support them in the opportunity.

We are often unfair to our newly appointed managers and directors when we promote them and just assume they will act exactly as the person before them or want them to come in and totally change everything ASAP. This is not who they are or should be. Invest in them. Coach them. Teach them. Send them for trainings. Let them discuss issues with you for guidance. Give them concrete things to work on and let them learn a best way to do it. DEVELOP them ... let's not wind them up and hope they run! Let's give them the tools they need to grow in this role!

POTATO CHIP LEADERSHIP SKILLS

WHO TRAINS YOUR BEST ASSETS?

You have three kids, all different ages. They are each on a different learning path. You work with each a different way. So why do we train levels of sales teams alike? Why do we bring aboard a trainer for a one-and-done, one-size-fits-all, and expect everyone to get what they need from it? And why do we do it once a year and say, "There, done."

Your biggest asset is your sales team. These are the revenue generators, the ones you should be investing in, as well as the leaders who lead them. These are the people who get the basic trainings from you and then advanced training from a next-level trainer who fits them.

Let's look at Inside Sales. These are your most raw sales members. Basics are crucial in their learning cycle: learning to make a call, what to say, how to get through objections, learning to deal with the dreaded "no," how to manage a call. This process starts with you as the leader, along with a valued member of your sales team. This gives that member the chance to grow. The sales trainer best for them will focus on establishing young sales reps, giving them the confidence to start their career, helping them believe in themselves, all while teaching the skill set necessary. They will continue to sell, so they can understand the challenges the young sales rep is going through in today's world. In a 9-month inside sales program, there should be continual sales training and hopefully one or two trainers developing skill sets.

Season, Premium, Group, and Corporate Account Executives. These are the reps who have excelled in the inside area and have moved up to a role with loftier goals, being there from a year or many more. We expect them to start setting appointments, meeting with companies, getting larger numbers in ... yet we still train them with a trainer who is highly skilled at developing the young sales rep establishing their career. For this group, we need to engage the trainer who will fine tune those skills and teach more about relationships (who are our people, where are our people, what are the needs of our people), influencing (how do we create a win atmosphere), challenging them to think in a more strategic way for accountability and planning, then executing these newly fine-tuned skills to a level of supersizing, anticipating, and—like a doctor—"diagnose and recommend." This sales trainer will be one who still helps to sell currently on a level of bulk season sales, premium sales, large group sales, and ideas for corporate, too. They will encourage reps to set meetings and give them the tools and confidence to find needs, assess, and recommend. They will enable the seasoned rep to hit the ground running after the training.

Then there are the fine-tuned reps who are more ready now for the art of negotiation and running a business at a high level. For this you need the high-end trainer, as results of these sales could be anywhere from a hundred thousand dollars to millions with naming rights. This is the trainer who works in depth with this unique, high-end group and creates more of an art of negotiating along with the strategizing.

The next part of the question is who (if anyone) is training your leaders? Are they flying by the seat of their pants or truly learning how to get the best out of their team, how to grow culture, how to be a servant leader, how to interview and find the right fit, how to evaluate in a productive way, how to create strategy, analyze existing sales, make recommendations? There are so many areas to leadership and so few educational opportunities we give them. Learning by trial and error is definitely not a win, but rather a loss for everyone. Time is wasted, trust is lost, frustration sets in and culture suffers.

I believe I speak for most sales trainers when I say, "assess your needs." Use us wisely. A successful department for you is a win for us. We want your department to excel. Question us. How much follow up do we provide? Which level do we find most success developing so that you hire us for the right fit? Which of us will provide the opportunity for your specific group to hit the ground running with a plan? You may find yourself hiring two or three trainers to maximize the levels of your biggest asset your company has ... your sales reps and your leaders. And that's ok! There is no "one size fits all." There should only be the right one at the right time for each group. Your trainings should reflect growth in training techniques with each level of your reps and leaders. *That's* how sales and leadership reps grow.

Teams who don't invest in training their sales staff to lead may never achieve their true potential and not learn other ways to use their strengths. Turnover is generally high as staff is no longer challenged and energized.

Take care of your biggest assets. Invest in them. Plan for the long term. It's easier to continue to invest than it is to start learning again, over and over and ...

POTATO CHIP LEADERSHIP SKILLS

WEAKNESSES OR STRENGTHS?

Do you have employees who seem to dread coming to work? Start out the day with little conversation? Have more negative than positive interactions with colleagues? Treat your customers poorly? Tell their friends they are miserable? Achieve increasingly less? Find that they have fewer creative moments? Clock watchers?

Companies who focus solely on "fixing" employees' weaknesses instead of enabling them to enhance their strengths will find that this only prevents failure—it doesn't build success. This is a huge difference. Focusing on the negative doesn't give us a chance to help grow the positive. The negative sticks out in the employee's mind. An employee is more apt to call in sick and become far less engaged in what is happening in the company when constantly reminded of shortcomings. Remember the days in school when you dreaded a class and would develop the infamous headache or stomachache so you could go to the school nurse during that hour?

As leaders, we have been trained in sports to fix things and fix people. We focus on the negative while trying to get to the positive. This creates a negative culture and thwarts engagement on the part of our staff. After all, if they have all these things that need fixing, why would they want to contribute an idea? It certainly wouldn't be worthy.

What if we, as companies, focused on each of our employee's strong points and enabled them to utilize those strong points? Focusing on building up your employee's individual strengths enables them to be more successful, have a more positive mind, and results in higher job satisfaction. They feel empowered and useful to the organization, and often will go above and beyond to offer more. It also enables them to not feel "beat up" when talking about how they can do better and are more apt to want to grow. Now you can help them improve in a far less threatening way. Phrasing their weakness as "how we can help you continue to grow" frames it in a more positive way, in which the account executive will be more receptive to the idea and to change. Employee engagement increases significantly.

Focusing on strengths with your employees enables teams to have purpose, focus on results, and prioritize what is best for the organization instead of what is best for only themselves. Most importantly, by focusing on strengths, your team becomes a magnet for talent. Hiring becomes easier as your pool of applicants as well as quality of applicants increases. People want to belong to an organization that helps them grow and has a "yes, we can" attitude. You are now attracting the talent you want.

THE THIRD CHIP

BRING YOUR TEAM INTO THE FUTURE

I had once written a blog about getting into sports. This led to an enormous amount of emails to me about getting out of sports. In one day alone, I heard from five people, four of whom are outstanding salespeople, who were leaving sports because, even though they reached their goals (three prior to the start of the season), they were written up because they did not conform to the correct number of calls per day, the only measure it seems our sales leaders have out there. I know there are teams out there who get it and would give a first-round draft pick to get these people to join their team. What is happening?

I am on a mission to train our sports sales leaders on how to lead going into the future—2020s, 2030s, and beyond. When I work with sales leaders and train, one of the areas we focus on is accountability and how we measure it. I guarantee 99% of them will say "number of calls per day and hustle board." My response to you as a leader: That theory on insanity is at work here. Doing the same thing year after year and expecting different results. We end up losing some of the best, and our turnover is horrendous.

As leaders, we need to have a general goal, general statement, and general expectations. But then we have to be realistic and realize that each of our reps are individuals. They learn differently, they hear differently, and most importantly, they have different strengths and will sell differently. If they hit their goal and it wasn't by a million calls a day but rather a more balanced menu of calls, meetings, social media, and more, is that a bad thing?

I dig deeper and ask why we think that way. Why do we measure accountability that way? The answers are very honest. It's the way we learned and the only way we know to measure. It's the way the VPs learned. If we don't continue it, we don't get promoted.

Sports has a lot more challenges than they did back in the '80s. At that time, sports entertainment was *the* thing in town … ballparks, courts, and arenas all were built with many suites added. It was the place to be seen and entertain. Then came the '90s and more entertainment opened. Now we are still mentally trying to justify the same methods that were used way back when.

I feel bad for so many who get promoted and are told, "Here's how I did it, just keep doing what you're doing," and the next thing we find is that that leader is frustrated, taking that frustration out on their staff, and failing as a leader. Their bosses want to look at call numbers, so we hyperfocus on that.

POTATO CHIP LEADERSHIP SKILLS

How do we break the cycle and how do we train our leaders differently? Do we even train our leaders? What should be focused on?

First and foremost, does your company/team have a training for Managers, Directors, VPs? They know how to lead in sales, as that is who we generally promote. But do they know how to coach? How to manage? If you have training, who does it? Internally or externally to present different ideas? Are they allowed to develop their style based on who they are and how they can best lead their team forward? Or are they told how to lead? The quickest way to let your new leader fail is to tell them how to manage. I once did a training with a team in which the coach of the team on the court tag-teamed with me. We created a dynamic presentation on how—be it on the court or off—to get the best out of your people.

Have they been taught how to assess individuals? Or are we still assuming everyone will be the same and expecting different results? Assessment skills and how to coach each individual is imperative to changing results.

Have they learned how to help their staff develop their individual business plans? This is not a single page. This is a well-thought-out plan for the quarter. I've had some that are 25 pages and some that are 5 pages. Have you trained your new leader on how/importance/coaching/assessment? If you have, are they using this as the measure of accountability? That is the whole purpose. Each sales rep is help accountable and coached through their own individual plan that *they* put together.

Put emphasis on talk time and quality conversations to find needs. We worry about call numbers to give our leaders, but why aren't we sharing and explaining to our supervisors the value of talk time? Are we having a quality conversation, building the relationship so we can move them up the pipeline with the ultimate goal of closing? If not, the plan of call volume isn't working. You should share that you watch talk time, not just call volume. Challenge them to get to know their prospect and their needs. Making a quality recommendation rather than throwing spaghetti against a wall and hoping it sticks is the way we should be teaching our staff.

What types of boards should be up? If revenue is the ultimate goal, then why focus on call volume as the main board or number of meetings? Send the message and focus on quality conversations and revenue, and get the competitive juices flowing as to how to get there. The problem is we focus so much on numbers that closing doesn't happen. We get the one hundred calls in. We get the ten meetings a week. We are managing numbers. The team should know the quarterly revenue and should set the daily revenue goal. Does the whiteboard show a Mendoza Line for each game? Do they know that that is the magic number at each game they cannot fall below? Do they know how to move someone up a pipeline? Do you have an experience board up so that those can be sold out before the season starts? As a leader, control what you can control. And what is that? You can control the *how* to get there, not the numbers.

Do we manage by intimidation or integration? Do we focus on what is not being done (not enough calls, not enough meetings, etc.) or do we focus on pulling the team together and having them set the daily goals and expectations and holding themselves accountable to them? Do we give coaching lessons to help them close, to help them use transition statements, and to help them understand strategy? Do we work with them individually on their strategic plan as to what is working, what is not? Is it the idea or the process? How can we improve the process? Generally an idea isn't bad, it's the execution part of our strategy. Are we asking their input and ideas as to how to get a weekly revenue goal hit? Our job as leaders isn't to manager numbers. It's to coach the process so all can hit those numbers.

Are we focusing on our leaders bringing in revenue or are we focusing on letting them manage? If we give them their own sales numbers to hit and keep hounding them to hit it, they get so focused on that portion that their team suffers. Gone is the coaching. Gone is the positive motivation. Gone is the empowerment. Instead it's: "Make calls so I can measure while I'm trying to get my numbers in." The leader's goal should not be equal to or above the staff. It should be an example goal that can be used to sit in on power hours and be part of the process.

Sales team leaders/Presidents/Owners: I implore you. Empower your people to break the mold. Let's create teams that use their gray matter and know how to bring in revenue and find ways to do it. Teams who will collectively come up with a plan for the week or quarter and go after it. I promise it will be a mix of ways, and *that's ok!* Actually, that's better than ok, as they are setting the foundation for the future. Let's stimulate that instead of punishing it. Let's stop having great staff leave and go into other industries where they are excelling because they are able to sell based on who they are and what they can bring to the table.

Our purpose should be one: to develop the sales reps and leaders of today to move us forward in the industry. They are the future of sports and entertainment. Let's believe in them and believe they have the passion and ideas to do things a little a differently than before. Then, as leaders, let's give them the tools to do it.

ARE WE THE REASON FOR THE EXODUS?

Working in sports definitely has its perks … working for something you are passionate about, the experience of being part of a team, helping our venues get filled. If that's the case, then why are quality people leaving? Clinging to an old philosophy does not bode well for the future.

Over the past few years, I have seen many excellent sales and service reps, as well as Managers and Directors, leave the industry where they excel to go somewhere else. Doing two intensive studies on this, the reasons are still the same after a two-year interval in between. Leadership (or lack of) and the communication that comes with it lead the pack. What are the areas we need to focus on when planning for leadership? How can we choose the person who will help break the mold of the problems? What are the ideas they have?

There are five groups of reasons why people are leaving that I have categorized. Does your leadership team recognize these? Are they working to change these? If not, how can we hire or promote people who will be the change agents who are needed?

Leadership:

- *Hiring reps that we feel are most like us and getting frustrated if they are not.* The key to success is not having a team of clones, but rather a team of varying strengths that can be brought to the table. One of the reasons reps cited for leaving was that the pressure to be like their leader and sell exactly like them was so great that it thwarted their ability to develop and be best at what they are hired for … selling.

- *Panic selling vs strategic selling.* Although most reps could have a strategic process to sales if shown how, oftentimes they end up with a team that produces "panic sales": selling game to game instead of a long-range plan. They are constantly having to focus on the upcoming game and are not able to create and use a sales process.

- *Lack of empowerment.* Reps feel that they have absolutely no say or ability to contribute to the ideas of the team; rather, they are told what and how to sell even though oftentimes it's clearly not what the customer wants.

- *Being told they spend too much time developing relationships instead of closing, closing, closing.* There is a fine balance here. For example, if you set a meeting, there is an expectation on the prospects side that you will ask for the close. However, if you are making calls, we have to grow our relationship more before we jump to close. These are the teams that have difficulty renewing clients, as they are selling for the short term and not the long term.

- *Staff is hitting goals, but you don't come in earlier than they do, even though the day may start at 8:30 am and some may come at 7 am.* Is dedication to the position measured by the hours put in or the results and commitment of the team to hit their goals? Hours are important in crunch time but are they expected year-round?

- *Hitting and exceeding goals but being reprimanded for inadequate call volume numbers.* This is beyond my comprehension. At this point, the rep has proven themselves and earned the right to run their own small business in the way that is successful for them. The key is they have earned it. Some are being reprimanded for using social media, which is a must in today's world. Some are being reprimanded for being out of the office, yet they are leading their team in sales because of in-person sales that they tend to do best.

- *Be put into a leadership position only to find no support system.* Congrats! You're in. Now make the team hit their goals. No guidance, no coaching, no mentoring. Manage by demotivation and numbers nightly because that is all you are being evaluated on. No help to understand the "how" to take them on the journey. Just make them sell.

- *Communication.* Nonexistent. Huge breaks in communication between organization, leadership, and staff. Is there a yearly meeting in which you present the company's past, present, and plans for the future? Are you having 1:1s (President to VPs, VPs to Directors, Directors to Managers, Managers to staff) weekly or at the very least biweekly?

Promised that growth would come from within, yet when positions open, continually hire from without. No point in staying when your evaluation is great but they want a "new voice" who ends up being their voice repeated again.

Lifestyle:

- *Imbalance in work/life.* Most reps today grew up with us as parents ... parents who were in the generation of working, working, working. Oftentimes, we parents missed school activities or games because of work. I tend to bring this up in discussion and it is amazing how many reps still feel that pain. These reps want more of a life balance and don't care to repeat our cycle. Can we blame them?

- *Didn't matter if goals were hit; still expected to come in early and stay late as "that's what you do in sports."* What is the incentive to working smarter or harder in the allotted 8 hours when you are still expected to stay? Management by hours is even worse than management by numbers. Are we using people or investing in people? There's a difference.

Diverse Disparity:

- *Disparity in pay.* Recently, in a two-month period, seven female Managers/Directors with Major League teams shared with me that they had been hired in or promoted for roles, finding afterward that they were hired anywhere from $18K to $35K less than male counterparts.

- *Perception that a female will leave once married.* I've had leaders tell me that they found a great candidate, only to find that they were either newly married or getting married, so they "probably won't be staying long so we didn't hire them."

- I was told by a VP from a Major League team that the team voted on me to do their training, but leadership felt it was owed to their male counterparts as "sports are more a guys thing" and they will "listen more to a guy than you."

- *Disparity in culture.* From reps being told that "our fans can't connect with you because of your different culture," to being hired to only take care of one specific market. From being promoted only to find it's not them that was believed in but rather to make sure they hit their required number of culture variances. Varying cultures creates culture. It sparks ideas. It gives insight as to how our customers view us, how varying customers relate, how customers live.

Pay:

- *Low base, low commission.* Graduating college, these kids today have huge loans to pay back. Yet we start them at or close to minimum, telling them they can make up with it by commission. That's true, they can. But a base barely above the poverty level upon graduating college is more apt to lose reps quickly (after we hopefully invested in them). Looking at our young reps, how can they make a rent payment, student loan payment, car payment, insurance payment, eat, have money for life's daily expectations, on the base given them? Sustainability is key. Teams such as the Minnesota Timberwolves and Lynx have broken the mold to create a more sustainable culture and create value for their team.

More will be covered later as to how to change this, but my question to you as a leader right now is whether you are contributing to their loss or finding ways to retain? How many times do we want to basic train over and over, year after year? Wouldn't we rather take an existing staff to new heights? How do I know the importance of my contribution as leader?

Potato Chip Trainers

Current Leaders with Leaders Under Us:

Coaching our mentees:

Time.

- Block time in your calendar weekly for coaching sessions for your mentees. These should not be business sessions, but rather true coaching sessions as to how to help them achieve success as a leader.

Use examples.

- Share times you did not choose wisely and times you did. You are human.

- How did you learn from mistakes?

Assist your mentee in time management.

- List three tips to manage their day, starting with day one.

- Identify daily steps to success.

- Identify coaching and assessing as the most important part of their day.

- Create a plan with them to make sure it happens daily.

- Build culture.

- Identify what good culture constitutes.

- With them, identify three steps to starting positive culture and how to develop these three steps.

- Identify ways to lead by example. Introduce one monthly.

- Example: have your mentee create 3 power hours each week on their calendar when they will sit down with their team and make calls.

- After power hour, encourage them to huddle and discuss, using these as coaching moments for your team.

- Training.

- Prior to promoting or hiring the leader, establish a training plan.

- In-house training plan:

- What will your weekly coaching session look like to introduce one training tip each week? Identify coaching steps you want to introduce.

- Identify how you will introduce each step.

- External training plan:

- Identify a training they can be sent to. Have it on the agenda. Identify the key tips you want as takeaways for them.

- Identify a trainer who can come in and train the leaders as a whole. Identify the key tips you want as takeaways from this.

- Identify three to five changes a training can bring and create time to discuss with your mentee how these changes can happen.

Current leaders, established and new:

Evaluate each rep:

- How does my staff learn?

- Meet with each individual and ask how each person best learns (hands on, reading, showing, etc).

- Make a list. Use this in coaching sessions so that you are communicating in the best possible way.

Identify my team's strengths:

- Write down each rep and, over the course of 2 weeks, list their top three strengths

- Identify their bottom three weaknesses

Create a coaching plan:

- How can I best coach their strengths for success?

- How can I coach them through the weaknesses to make them more successful?

What is my communication style?

- Sales communication is 80/20: 80 from the client, 20 from us.

- Evaluate our own communication. Are doing most of the talking?

- Make a list of each meeting/coaching session. How can you talk less?

- Delegation.

- Create what your to-do list looks like.

- Identify which are most important in developing your staff.

- What is left on your list? How much can be delegated as a growth opportunity?

- For example, coaching sessions are crucial. Evaluating numbers and how to get there is important but can be a combined effort. How can you combine it? Collecting the data is not crucial to your job as leader. Who can collect the data daily?

- Another example. We tend to "own" the whiteboards. Coaching them on the why of what is on the whiteboard and brainstorming the how to get there is crucial. Writing on them yourself is not. Letting go of the whiteboards and letting staff manage them creates accountability for where they are and where they need to be.

Identify how we can best let them be part of the business. Create more engagement.

- Questions and Answers

- Be part of the solution, not the problem.

- Plan time daily on your calendar to answer questions that need answering.

- Waiting for answers says, "My needs and clients aren't important."

- Create a half hour to 45 minutes daily either for staff to sit down and discuss questions that need answering or spend the time answering those questions sent to you.

- Make a decision. Unless it's earth shattering, make a decision.

Assess:

Learn assessment techniques.

- Situational projects.

- Assign a project.

- Identify: where are they strongest in the process?

- Where do they struggle?

- Areas they struggle are added to your coaching list.

- Have your team be part of new hires process.

- Coach them as to what to be looking for as they are with them.

- Your team learns leadership skills and you learn what a potential new hire is like away from leadership.

- Eliminating turnover:

Identify each area of why staff leaves and how you can improve it currently.

Leadership and Communication

Have staff repeat your communication back to you in coaching session. Are they hearing what you are saying?

Work/Life Balance

Have staff members create Outlook calendar items before they leave each day including their call list for next day. Fulfill their day, leave with clear conscience.

Diversity

Create a culture day each month. Have a different rep bring in a sampling of food or experience of their culture. Hire quality, not a body—no matter race, creed, ethnicity, etc. Their contributions often will be a great learning experience for the entire staff.

Pay

Opt for surprise bonuses for above and beyond.

The Fourth
Potato Chip

FULL STAFF ENGAGEMENT

Do you feel you are doing a great job communicating and engaging with your staff?

Answer these questions:

- I spend 80% of my day in my office or at my desk not communicating with my team except through email.

- I have weekly meetings where everything gets discussed.

- I coach 1:1s and, for lack of anything better to discuss, we discuss pipelines and call volumes.

Does this sound like you? If so, you're a victim of the "ivory tower" philosophy. In this philosophy, leaders are so focused on managing numbers that they forget they are there to coach their people.

Let's look at some of our areas of potential engagement and see where we can improve.

Continual vs weekly. If you feel that a weekly engagement is enough and you then let them go at it, you are missing the opportunity to grow your staff so they can reach great numbers. Continual engagement is not micromanaging. It's being part of the process. I'm not saying you should be talking to them the whole time, but I am saying that being out of the ivory office tower will help you do continual coaching rather than once a week. For those of us with kids, we know that to coach them when they do something has meaning. To coach them 3 days later about something means absolutely nothing to them. Do you sit on power hours during the week? Do you coach the reps during? Teachable moments. Priceless.

In your ivory tower or with the staff? If you are managing by walking around, you

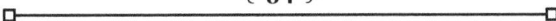

know how conversations are going, what closing techniques they are using, how they are managing their time, etc. When you do this, you are able to make that 1:1 coaching session so much stronger. How do you know what to meet with them about if you are not in the room with them? You are managing numbers and the numbers will never come.

Schedule time. More important than scheduling time is keeping it available. Nothing is worse than scheduling a 1:1 with your team member and continually changing because you have deadlines. The most important job you have is to coach your team. Nothing else should take precedent. If you commit to coaching, the team will grow and so will your numbers and reputation. Blocking out your calendar as 'busy' sends the message to everyone else in the organization that your team is the most important part of your week. Respect grows.

Identify the best time to coach. When the staff is fried at the end of the day, why would we have our 1:1 coaching then? Do we really think they are listening? When is the team freshest? Generally, the morning. Schedule them for half-hour intervals on the same day every week, starting first thing in the morning. Have them come prepared and, more importantly, you come prepared. Know how you can best help them grow during the next two measurable weeks.

Sell in front of them. One of the best lessons you can share with your staff is the art of selling. Telling them is one thing. Showing is another. Schedule yourself to sit in on three power hours a week and make calls yourself. Let them know that even you can mess up. What is important is how you fix it. They need to know that you are human, you can sell, and which techniques have been successful for you.

You can't win them all. There will always be someone that you have a harder time engaging with. That's ok. Your job is to learn about your staff, learn what excites them, learn how they sell, and learn how they learn. Once you find out who they really are, you will start winning them one at a time. It's a process. There has to be trust. Trust comes when a relationship is developed. Take your time and do it right.

Why is engagement important?

Getting to know our staff and truly engaging with them reduces turnover. It also improves their ability to sell as they feel more a part of the process and the team. This leads to a better culture, in which we retain more customers and increase revenue. When employees and leaders engage, the team is happier overall and the salesroom becomes high energy. This is starting a great culture!

THE FOURTH CHIP

THE "DREADED" MEETINGS

There is an old saying: Those who enjoy meetings should never be in charge of anything.

A common thread I am starting to hear is, "We spend more time in meetings that keep getting called than we do actually selling or trying to set meetings with clients."

When asked what the meetings are about, the answers vary:

We just changed the sales process ... again.

- Kneejerk: we need to increase sales, so we are going to focus on trying this *right now.*

- Stop what you are doing ... we need to shift gears.

- Here's how we are going to sell ____ now.

- Here's another package "we" created.

- You're not getting enough calls in a day.

- We want to motivate you to do better.

- And the list goes on ...

Even worse are the meetings we create to focus on numbers instead of the process. If your team is called together frequently to discuss the numbers and never coaching on the process, it is another wasted meeting instead of an opportunity.

Think about this: you have one tank of gas and it has to last you all week. Are you going to run to the store every time you need one item or collect your list and make one smart trip, thus leaving additional gas for other ventures?

Our sales reps have one tank of gas in them each day. We expect them to make their kazillion calls, set appointments, be on the road, have in-person meetings, sell via social media, take calls, and oh, by the way, we are calling a couple of extra meetings today. The sad thing is that they leave the meeting thinking, "Why on earth did we just sit through that?"

As a sales rep, our people want to be part of the process. But being part of the process does not mean calling a lot of meetings. What it does mean is the meeting you host should have substance, with a clear reason to be called, and yield valuable input.

So how often should you meet as a team or individuals? Two meetings a week is a lot … any more than that and we are actually trying to do some work in between the work of meetings. What are the most important meetings?

There are three areas:

- The morning huddle.

- This is not a traditional meeting but rather a huddle held by your staff daily the moment your day begins.

- A biweekly sales meeting and a biweekly coaching meeting.

- Held on opposite weeks, these two meetings are the nuts and bolts of your department.

- The sales meeting should be one run more by your team and the coaching meeting is your opportunity to grow your staff.

- How should these three key areas be managed?

Morning huddle: This should be led by staff members, a different member each week, and should last about 3 minutes. Any more than that and it's another dreaded meeting. The 3-minute huddle includes: sales tip, timing of the day's power hours, revenue goal for the day … all set by the staff. *At this time, if there is something important to add, you can add two minutes and share it. A 20-minute morning huddle is not a huddle … it is another dreaded meeting.*

1:1s: A 1:1 every week or every other week is a necessary use of time. This is a good time to share something that came up that particular week. If it's not an emergency, share it during this time. These are your coaching sessions. This is your time to coach the staff member on a measurable technique that they can grow into and put into practice.

The 1:1s should also be a discussion of their business strategy (you strategized three in-person appointments per week this month … tell me more about those meetings and how they are going) and not the same questions every other week (who is in your pipeline, what do you think will close, etc).

The biweekly sales meeting held opposite the 1:1s: This should never be a numbers meeting and yet that's what they turn into. We manage numbers. We aren't controlling what we can control. Why aren't we managing *people?* This is a meeting that is team run. The team should be prepared to present where they are in the process of their sales: the planning phase (who and what), the building phase, and the "who is ready to move in" phase. This is the pipeline broken down into reality for the team. The team then decides what is the best way they can focus on the revenue goal for the next two weeks. *This is no longer a managing-by-numbers game, but rather the staff managing goals/expectations and setting measurable results with them.* There should also be a short sales training in this meeting either by you or by a member of the sales team. *And then, as leader, YOU have the floor at the end to share any new info or brainstorming session or whatever you want to add.* It is important to remember the 80/20 rule in sales—it applies here, too. Let your staff do 80% of the energized talking and planning. Now they are part of the process, which is key. They feel more involved in the business. In a sense, they are running their business with your guidance.

When you think about all the meetings that are called, honestly ask yourself how many are that important? How many can be condensed to a few minutes and added to an existing time of day when everyone gathers, thus not continually interrupting our sales reps' day?

Our reps need to be set up for success. As leaders, we need to do that by managing how much we tend to interfere with their day. We need to give them the time to accomplish their goals. It's hard enough sometimes to get into that groove of repetition when calling. Constant interruptions caused by additional meetings will never enable them to get into the groove!

Sometimes meetings become the practical alternative to work! Are you making this happen to your staff!

POTATO CHIP LEADERSHIP SKILLS

RUNNING YOUR SMALL BUSINESS MEETINGS

We have the three types of meetings that make the business run. How about the meetings that get the staff vested in the business? These are the meetings that fuel the fire of energy for the team if held correctly. There are two kinds of these meetings: the quarterly and the year-end/start meetings.

Quarterly meetings (the first by leadership, thereafter by a quarterly team leader):

- What is the revenue goal that needs to be hit for the quarter? Have the team brainstorm the how/who they will approach to hit this goal.

- Brainstorm with the team what they feel are the most important areas for sales/retention for the quarter.

- Have the staff vote on the two areas they feel they need to focus on the most (example, selling 100 season club seats, $___ in group deposits)

- Focusing on what they voted on for the quarter, what will be the call/in person patterns? What will be the strategy? What will be the categories? This is for the team to brainstorm and create with your guidance.

- The meeting should end with a solid, trackable plan.

- Who will be the team leader for this quarter? Focus on revenue, set a chart, inspire/motivate, send out sales rep of the week, etc. This is an opportunity for each rep to learn leadership and what it takes to motivate and coach a staff.

45 days into the quarter:

- Where are they in relation to goal?

- What are the challenges?

- Collectively decide what needs to be done to hit goals.

- The meeting should end with a solid plan that is trackable.

Year-end/start meetings:

There should always be two year-end events: The Energizing Meeting and the Celebratory Meetings.

The Energizing Meeting

Two-day session; season/premium, group, CP, marketing, box office

First day: The Starting Point

- ***The first topic is a state of the union address.*** This should be a yearly detailed look at the business … where it was 5 years ago, where it is today, and the ideas the organization has for it over the next 5 years.

- ***This is a crucial meeting for the staff to feel part of the business and take ownership of what it is they need to do to be part of the vision.***

After looking at the past and the future, concentrate on the present. What is in store for this year? How will we achieve it?

The process: What worked well this past year, what didn't? Was it the idea or the execution?

Brainstorm on how you can capitalize on what worked and then brainstorm on what you need to improve on the process for those that didn't work as well.

Go through each department and look at the pluses and minuses for the year, evaluating how you can capitalize on what worked and brainstorm each for how to improve those that didn't.

Second day: Creating something new

- Brainstorm ideas for upcoming season for all departments.

- Brainstorming new supersize groups.

- Plan goals as a team.

- Strategize new ideas to bring in business, new concepts, new events.

- Create the how/why and expectations.

- Upon leaving day two:

- Overall plan as to what the year will look like for each department:

- Goals

- Strategies

- New concepts

- Everyone's commitment

The Celebratory Meetings

Academy Awards Event: Celebratory end-of-the-year event

Invitations should be equivalent to the Oscars, invite should include team member and their guest.

- Event includes dinner and program.

- From the moment the team walks in, they enter the red carpet with stars with their name on the floor and intern "paparazzi" taking their pictures behind a golden backdrop.

- Fun emcee for the event. Categories to include:

- Rookie of the Year

- Third/Second/First place sales (groups, season, premium, corporate)

- Award for most revenue in each category (groups, season, premium, corporate)

- Award for most overall revenue

- Award for most improved

- Year start meetings

- Kickoff to the season in conjunction with hitting a goal:

- Goal should be set at end of season to be attained by a month before opening.

- When goal is achieved the kickoff to the season is held about 2 weeks before opening day.

- This should be a rah-rah, high-energy, fun event but focused on celebrating a job well done.

Example: Decorate for a luau around a bar area and have an afternoon luau with a toast to the upcoming season, thanking them for work so far and focusing on goal left to attain.

What is the result of this type of structure?

Focus: the staff becomes focused on attaining goals vs catching up.

Positive vs negative: this is a more positive way to run the business vs constantly talking about call volume, revenue, and pipeline.

Better direction: the staff now has guided direction vs dialing for dollars. They are part of the process and truly feel a part of the business rather than simply being bodies to make calls.

Tactics vs numbers: in this way, you as leader can control what you can control … the methods to success vs controlling numbers.

It is one thing to go to meetings three and four times a week where all that is discussed is the subject of meetings! It is another to host specific event meetings in which the staff feels a part of the business and is energized and takes ownership. This is the start of staff involvement. This ends the mounds of meetings and creates an empowered staff.

POTATO CHIP LEADERSHIP SKILLS

STOP RUNNING YOUR SALES MEETINGS

What does your sales meeting look like? Do you give them numbers and totals? Do you ask what they have in the pipeline coming up? Do you tell them what goals they need to hit? Do you go over call volume? Do you tell them what is coming up next to sell and how it will be sold? Do you tell them your expectations till the next sales meeting? My, aren't we telling them a lot? What happened to the 80/20 rule in sales?

Does your staff have that glazed look? Do they look at you but you feel they are really not listening? Are they doing 20% of the talking or less? Did you notice in the above paragraph how much that meeting has revolved around you?

If so, STOP! It's time to change these meetings!

You are doing exactly what a leader should NOT be doing ... *telling, setting their expectations, making all the decisions.*

As a leader, it's not up to you to give all the info, set all the expectations, tell them what to work on.

As a leader, you are the coach. You should be coaching them in 1:1s, role playing, providing individual help so they can become the best they can be.

Build the visionary plan and the upcoming strategy for the department. Coaching *them,* not numbers. In a sales meeting, you should be *empowering and giving ownership.*

What should a sales meeting look like?

1. *Sales meetings should be owned by the sales team.* This is engagement.

2. *Different sales member has ownership of the meeting(s) for the month.* This is their opportunity to lead and develop.

3. *The meeting should consist of a learning component.* The leader of the month can assign someone who will be responsible for teaching an aspect of sales that everyone could brush up on and presenting it in any manner they want. They have 15 minutes of your sales hour to provide a priceless teaching moment.

4. *The meeting should consist of the leader asking the team what areas they feel need to be focused on the most.* A list should be made on a whiteboard.

5. *The team should vote on the two things they feel most necessary to focus on for the month.* Once they vote on the "what," they then set their goal for it and the "how." This consists of brainstorming how they can best accomplish the goals. They decide who will cover what, and how. They work together as a team.

Someone is asked to volunteer as the team lead for the focus. That is the person who will check in with you as to what is being accomplished weekly.

1. *Subsequent meetings during the month are focused again on how/who and other ways to achieve the focus goals.* Planning. Executing. What is working? What is not? How can they adapt? Do you realize this is leadership in action? This is how they learn to lead … by learning how to solve problems, strategize a plan, and then execute.

2. *What is your role?* Okay, you ARE the leader and we don't want to totally forget you. You can have *no more* than 5 minutes to talk about anything new that is happening. If it's a new package that you want to unroll, announce it. But from there, *let the team develop it and add the "how" they will go about introducing it, selling it, etc.*

Can you see where this would create a most engaging team? A team who takes ownership of the focus, ownership of the strategy and execution, and ownership of their sales. A team who is learning how to grow and develop on the job instead of lip service?

Much like the quarterly meeting, staff is learning to identify what is most important for focus as well as the strategy to accomplish it. This is invaluable to their growth and helps the organization move forward as a whole. You are no longer "telling" and being the sole voice, but rather it is now a team effort that is engaging and communicative.

Get more by letting go. You hired them. Now trust them. It's time for them to show what they can do.

POTATO CHIP LEADERSHIP SKILLS

RETAINING A SUCCESSFUL TEAM

Sometimes a sales team is constant and you can continue to work with and grow them throughout the year. Other times, it's a revolving door as we discussed earlier. The question is, knowing why staff members leave sports, how do we keep them?

Telling vs asking. If you go into work and are told what to sell, how to sell, everything is already done and all you do is call, call, call, how excited are you? Create ownership and empower your reps to create ideas. Let them be part of the process.

Afraid of social media. If we don't fully understand something as leaders, it's our job to learn more about it. Social media is one of the methods of today's sales and many reps are doing well with it. Learn about it. Find out how they are being successful at it. Let them teach you.

Usage of video. 67% of videos are opened compared to 33% of emails. Don't be afraid of letting your reps create personal videos of touchpoints to send their prospects as well as their clients. Use what works.

Promotions. Promotions are meant to be for those ready for the next step, those who are proving themselves in areas beyond just selling. Know your staff. Are they helping without asking? Are they taking initiative? Do they take ownership of projects and return by the due date without follow up on your part? Do they mentor their peers?

Invest. In both your leaders and your staff. Show them their value by investing in them.

Open yourself to change. Why is it so many leaders are threatened by a younger generation? It seems that we are uncomfortable with their mindset, their desire to keep learning, to be part of the process, to offer ideas, and (gasp!) use their brain.

Times have changed. They want to know the "why." Present the future. Present the why. Let them be part of the process. They will then invest in your business.

Engagement. Empowerment. Ownership. It's not *your* business. It's not your owners' business. It belongs to every single person who works there. Empower them to be part of it. Engage them in conversations and brainstorming. Give them ownership of projects to grow.

Interview intelligently. Are we seeing what they truly have to offer or are we looking for them to fit a mold? Are both of you asking the right questions? Do you understand their needs and wants prior to coming onboard so there are no surprises?

Paycheck reality. Create a base pay that enables your staff member/leader to survive. Ask yourself: Will this base enable them to rent an apartment, pay car insurance, utilities, eat, and pay off student loans? The commission should be the bonus for the extras.

In sales we say it's three times harder to get a new customer than to keep an old one, and yet we don't apply that same rule to our staff. Are we working to keep them or checking boxes? As long as the door keeps revolving, the people who lose the most are our clients. Let's put new doors up that make it harder to get in because no one wants to leave. That consistency will help our staff, our company, and, above all, our clients.

Potato Chip Trainers

Practice the first step to engagement: leave your office

- Over the next two weeks, create a new habit. Leave your office once in the morning and once in the afternoon and walk into the sales room(s), engaging with the staff by name.

Creating a coaching timeline.

- Construct your calendar with a time each morning every other week for 1:1 coaching. Set the time up with each member. About 99% of the time, make sure these are nonnegotiable times. This way, you will be committed to their growth.

- Set your calendar for two blocks during the week, in which you will go into the salesroom and sit in on power hours, listening to each of the reps. This is your chance to coach on the spot.

Create morning energy.

- If you don't have a 3-minute morning huddle, start one. Assign a rep to run the first week, then they pick the rep for the next, etc. Three things covered in a huddle: sales tip for the day, power hours set, sales revenue goal established.

Let go of the sales meetings.

- Outline questions for engagement and have the staff do 80% of the talking. Following meeting, assign a rep to run it.

Have the staff establish a quarterly strategy.

- Enable them to brainstorm, then write their individual plans. Have them present to you.

Listen.

- Listen to your staff. Encourage new ideas. Review ideas with them. Let them go after their ideas. Don't be afraid to empower. If you're not sold out every game, you need to be open to new ideas.

The Fifth
Potato Chip

ABBA HAD IT RIGHT... TAKE A CHANCE ON HIRING

You go to school. You get a degree because the job requirements say you have to (not always sure why). You are ready for your first job in sports. And then … you end up working for a manufacturing company, a restaurant, or an insurance company. Great companies, but what happened to the goal? Where did it go and how did it not happen?

You have a stellar background. You apply. They like you. And then nothing. Why? "A little too qualified for us." Okay … if you're not 100% sold out, maybe it's time to think a little differently.

As I travel the country working with teams, I find some interesting hiring habits and strategies. I'd like to examine a few of these and ask that you think about your own experiences.

We want an Ivy League school grad. Please explain the difference to me between someone who has gone to "small town USA" college or top-of-the-line major college? What's more important in the hiring process, where they went or what they accomplished while in school? I am far more willing to take a chance on a kid who went to any college, had to work their way through, plus took full-time courses and still participated in community events and/or school events and internships. This is a person who knows time management, has need, and motivation. Great start for a first job. I don't care where you went, just tell me about your experience and work while there.

College degree only. We miss a lot of quality sales reps, operations managers, and great youth coaches that could be selling very well on some of our teams by only looking at the degree. Those teams that offer the comment "or similar experience" often find staff members who are in the community selling news ads, radio ads, doing B2B sales already, managing operations at companies, some with and some without a degree. Think about them. Don't just write them off. (By the way, I went to a diploma program at a nursing school … which is not a bachelor's degree. I don't think I turned out too bad in sales!).

We've narrowed it down to a couple candidates and you are one; you find out later the other is in house. So many times this is the kiss of death to a candidate. How often have you, as a team, gone through the process just in case someone is better but honestly knowing in your heart you are giving it to the in house person? Why carry it so far? Why give that other candidate hope if you know how it will end up? Free them up to get a position elsewhere.

We're looking for someone who can make an immediate impact. Someone who is not afraid to sell B2B, meet execs, etc. You hire them. And what do you have them do? "Well, I can't really have any measure if you are out on the road, so we need you to stay and make a hundred calls a day." The immediate impact has just been deflated. You are taking someone with strong talents in areas you asked for and asking them to redesign completely that which made them successful, more often than not so that you can have a measure of activity. Base it on success. If it's not working, then make the recommendation. But give them the chance to do what you originally asked them to do and be successful at it.

Yes, you sell very well and meet with a lot of CEOs. Yes, we know you have also sold premium very well. Yes, we know your next step is a desire to conquer sponsorship sales. But we can't do that unless you have sponsorship experience. What?? Two words: *grow* and *develop*. How many of our teams have that wording in their philosophy, on their job site, in their job description, yet the staff will tell you it never happens? Let's put into action what we say.

We know social selling is important, but we leave that up to marketing (ie, we're not sure what you are doing during the day on social media, so we'd rather you not use it). Younger sales members nowadays see the value in social media. They see the value of adding season ticket holders and group leaders to a separate Facebook account of theirs that caters to the sport more, or Snapchat, or Instagram. They talk with clients to see their preferred method of communication … Emails? Calls? Texts? In person? I've had reps who have exceeded sales goals by the influx of sales from social media offers/comments. They are using video wisely. Be sure of what they are doing by *learning* what they are doing. They can help us grow as much as we can help them.

You really seem to be our candidate … we'll connect next week. Then, crickets. What happened? Whether promoting from within, finding another candidate, or simply deciding not to hire period, have the courtesy of letting the person know. Respect their time as you would want them to respect yours. Free them up for another opportunity instead of destroying self-confidence trying to figure out what happened, or worse, having them chase you because you aren't comfortable following up.

On the other hand, you hear, "Yes, you would make a great coordinator/ manager/director … and we say we promote from within but continually promote from without. "You're just not quite ready yet. We will get someone with more experience." Our job is not to put them in the position and walk away. Our job is to continue to grow them and develop them when we put them in that position. It's not just on them, it's also on us as leaders. I've had many reps say, "Why bother anymore? They will never hire from within," and then leave the team or sports entirely, and end up truly excelling somewhere else.

The Abba song "Take a Chance on Me" comes to mind. I have mentored so many people that could truly make a great impact on a team but won't be looked at because of the profile we have set up and won't budge from. I had one kid who sent a letter to a team President and said he would scrub floors if he had to just to get in and prove himself. We shouldn't have to make it that hard. (By the way, that kid was brought in and worked harder than anyone, and no, he wasn't scrubbing floors).

There are some excellent teams out there who understand and truly grow and develop their people. The culture is a thriving one. Teams such as the El Paso Chihuahuas, where teamwork and focusing on growing their people and keeping them happy are key. Again, it's the result of the right management from top down there, with Alan Ledford, Brad Taylor, and Nick Seckerson. Another great example is a team such as the Trailblazers, where Joe Isse takes great pride in teaching his staff, developing them, and having them immediately ready for the next role, where they will provide excellent results with a seamless transition.

Let's not narrow our field of candidates entirely according to what we have put down on paper, but rather be open minded to those out there who may be able to make that immediate impact. Sadly, we've discounted them because of where they went to school, if they went to school, if they are too social media savvy, or if they have a desire to take that next step or they don't fit the mold we've created. Let's not create a mold. Let's let Abba lead us to "Take a Chance."

HIRING THE BEST

How often have you hired someone, only to find 3 months later that you may have made a big mistake? You ran the ad, asked the questions, had your team look at them, and everybody said sure. So, what happened?

There should be a career out there for good interviewees. They've read the book, answer well, but really can't work well. But boy, can they interview well! How many times has this happened to you?

Did you define beforehand:

- What is it you were looking for in the hiring process? The strengths needed? Someone who easily builds relationships? Someone with the right attitude? Someone who can influence? Someone who can strategically think?

- What are the questions you are asking? Are they straight out of a book, or the "cute" questions employers now ask? Or are they thought-provoking questions to get to know how the person thinks, reacts, and believes? Questions that get to the heart of the person?

- What is it that is missing from your team that could enhance it? This is crucial. Is the team really good at creating ideas but can't seem to execute them? Is it a team that has a hard time closing? A team that hates to be out of the office meeting new people and would rather just stay by the phone? Does your team mix their day with social media or shy away from it?

- Does it really matter what their major was or if they even went to college? What is the real reason you are insisting on college only? In preparing for interviews, I often ask the candidate to prepare examples of their experience in the areas specified.

- Observe people you meet with businesses you support every day, from the grocers to the cleaners to where you buy your clothes to how they handle people at your local fast food restaurant … they may just be your next hire.

In sales, we focus on finding needs. Then why in sports sales interviewing do we *fill positions* instead of *filling needs*. Why aren't we following the same process when interviewing?

How can we hire smarter?

Take time to sit down and write up the strengths and qualities you are looking for in the candidate instead of looking at other teams and using their job descriptions. That is THEIR team. What about YOURS? How often do we just send out the typical request for sales reps that we've been sending for the past 10 years? Good attitude, college graduate, wants to be in sales, blah blah blah. What is it you really want to round out your team? Are you looking for someone who is a strong influencer? Someone who can create a strategy plan? Someone who also understands the social side of selling well? Define what it is that will enhance your team. Do you want creativity? Do you want someone who closes best in person? Do you want someone comfortable in meetings? Have them prepared to give you samples of when they were most creative and the results. This is what you are looking for.

If you are looking for a sales rep, why are you only looking at college grads? Some of my smartest hires came when I went somewhere and had someone sell something to me. Watching them in action with others, handling difficulties, then selling to me. I simply ask, "Would you ever be interested in selling in sports?" Some of the best premium and corporate sellers came from someone I saw in action. You can see firsthand how they handle challenges, how they recommend, how they influence, their overall demeanor.

What is it they can bring to the table? Are you asking questions that help you find their skill set? Questions that help you see if they will fit the culture? Questions that test if they are strong in influencing? Strategic planning? Relationship building? If you are asking standard interview questions, you will most likely get a standard employee, one who has memorized the interview book. Ask those that get to the heart of the person, that help you know how they react in situations— questions that make them think and share their real self with you.

What is the most important quality to find in hiring? Attitude. It's either good or bad. You can teach sales. You can help teach strategy. But you can't teach attitude. Make sure you hire the right attitude.

Are you looking for a mini-you? If so, that's not a good hire. A department of clones of the leader will not be a great culture mix. It will not be a team that works together cohesively. It is not a team that will collaborate. It will be a team who is constantly vying for your attention to be that "next one."

We get hundreds of resumes, largely because we really don't define who we want. We often miss the right person because we generalize so much. I once ran an ad that asked for someone who had experience in the service industry, from bank tellers, to servers, to hotel employees. It was one of the best periods of hiring I ever had. I hired people already used to working to satisfy their clients, people who were used to having people get angry with them, people who knew how to use transition statements to make the client happy.

As a leader, hiring is one of the most important responsibilities you will have. You won't be managing numbers, you will be coaching people to help them hit those numbers. Before you run that ad or ask that recruiter, know what it is you are looking for. Sometimes the best people are those you would least expect, mainly because we didn't take the time to look beyond the resume and find the real person inside.

THE FIFTH CHIP

WHO DO YOU HIRE IN SALES?

You send out the notice. You get five to five hundred applications. You *have* to hire someone. You are minus "a body." Who do you hire?

As a leader, you know that you are only as good as the people around you. Ultimately, you want to hire someone who is actually better than you and can bring more new business aboard. How do you help fine tune them? How do we create a hiring process? How can we find a "solid" member with key strengths to convert to a ticket department sales mentality?

Forget hiring a body and start looking at everybody. Some of the best talent I have brought aboard was found at an ice cream shop, a rental car business, a hospital, and a shoe store. I am constantly looking for great talent. We should never stop. We shouldn't limit ourselves to a bunch of resumes or just hiring anyone to fill a quota and hoping they swim and not sink. The word sales means "to serve," so we need someone who understands the servicing of a client as well as the selling. With a little guidance, they will also become a stellar sales person. In serving, they already understand the importance of the needs of the client and how to fulfill those needs. They can take that same philosophy to our sales department.

If they've had team sales experience, dig deeper in the conversation. Are they open to more than one way to sell? Are they open to change … as change is strong from one team to another? On the flip side, what can they bring that would enhance the current culture? In essence, how can they make the department better? Or do you simply want someone to come in and sell from day one? What happens if they only know one process and aren't open to learning others? Are they coachable? Did you find that out?

Interview with more than basic questions and "cute" textbook questions. Ask thoughtful questions based on the four areas of strengths, and you will quickly know a) where they will need additional training, and if you will have the time to do the type of training needed for that area, b) if they have the needed traits to be successful, and c) what type of onboarding would be most successful for them. Customize your onboarding.

POTATO CHIP LEADERSHIP SKILLS

Look beyond the name of the college. I have had some teams who want most of their hires to come from elite colleges. Many of them ask analytical questions to assess their thinking ability. All well and good but give me someone who had to work their way through college … someone who went full time and also held down a job. This is a person who knows they have to build relationships and that they have goals they need to hit to be able to pay for school as well as make it through school. This is a person who is not afraid to do what it takes to get the job done. This is also a person who is going to work hard for those commissions.

Do we look for people just like us? Is that more of our comfort zone? If so, we are doing the organization a huge disservice. Fresh ideas, animated culture, and true collaboration comes from hiring talented people who are NOT clones of us. Every team, somewhere in their mission statements or department statements or disclosure statements, comments that they believe in a diverse culture. But do they? If we hire only people just like us, then how diverse is it? How much creativity is sparked? Is culture alive and going off like fireworks?

Are we looking for people who truly want to sell or people we hope to convert to sell? Often we are in such haste to fill that seat with a warm body, we fill it with someone we think we can simply convert to sell. How often does that work? Take the time to find people who really want to sell. This should be a major qualifier. I am finding more and more students reaching out to me saying that they want to go the sales route. I have people in the workforce who tell me they just want to be able to go to a job and sell. These are the people we should be looking for. Playing on a sport team and understanding teamwork and hard work is one thing but wanting to become a salesperson is another.

Have the team members interview some of the finalists also. Ask your team what they value most in their culture. Help them learn how to spot qualifiers for this. Have them observe areas such as: attraction or distraction? Do they listen or mostly talk? How do they manage their conversations? Are they inclusive to all people or exclude others as they answer to one. Giving your staff solid areas to look for enables them to grow as leaders and also gives them the chance to observe the candidate in a large group setting. They have to be the ones to work with this person every day; they should have the opportunity to at least help evaluate key areas. This will also give you a broader picture of the candidate. The staff doesn't have to have the final say, but conversation around pros and cons and why or why not can be both enlightening and offer growth to the team as well as to you.

Hiring should never be a process of asking questions/getting answers. It should be more of a process of observation, assessment, and an understanding of what it will take to get this person to that next level. Interviewing in the hiring process should come with an assessment sheet of understanding your job once this person would be hired. You assess/strategize your ticket sales department; why not the candidates you are interviewing? Don't look for "the body" ... look for the heart and soul of someone who wants to succeed and grow. What will be your investment?

There is nothing better and more successful than a culture of a mix of people who have strong strengths and are coached, taught, encouraged, and empowered. It all starts with who you hire.

POTATO CHIP LEADERSHIP SKILLS

INTERVIEWING YOUR FUTURE TEAMMATES

More and more graduates are contacting me to let me know that they want to be in a sales role. Many in sales are looking to grow. Some are ready to start their first, second, or farther up leadership role. Most ask what is the best first step or what is the best next step? The question for them is: What is it you want?

The key to a sports sales or leadership job is in interviewing the interviewer. What exactly is happening in the conversation? Are they "selling you" on the position? Is it about why it is the best? Or is it about understanding you?

In sales, it's all about the customer. Why should it be any different when interviewing? When my daughter was going off to college, she became quite good at interviewing those she was interviewing with. I remember when she visited one prestigious college in the area and, while the school's Vice President was busy selling her on the college, she simply asked, "What are you going to do to help me be successful in my future career?" He went back to selling her on the college. She responded with, "I learn best in a smaller environment where I get to know my teachers and can ask for help if I need it. Am I one of many or am I considered an individual who wants to learn? If I get stuck, will someone coach me if I reach out?" Needless to say, she didn't end up going there. Not because of her questions, but because he couldn't come up with answers.

Let's look at your interview. There's the usual: tell me about yourself. Why should you have this position? Why should we invest in you? And in some instances, a video is required to make sure you can walk and chew gum at the same time. And then you get accepted or rejected. Somewhere in there they asked if you had questions. What do you ask? How do you ask it? What is most important to you?

On the flip side, you go in headstrong for all the wrong reasons. This is not a recipe for success, but rather a recipe for failure on your side and the team side. Know why you are going into this as a career. "I'm starting in sales so I can get into Community Relations," will not endear you. Your opportunities to switch will most likely not be there in today's sports world. Each area is its own. If you are going into sales, go into it to be a true salesperson. Build your career on it, as they will spend time and money growing you. If you want to be in marketing, then ask what it takes to get into a marketing role. Most teams want someone with 3 to 5 years of experience, so perhaps you will be working in college marketing or an advertising agency to gain those years of experience. Take the steps you need to define the career you want.

Applying for a leadership role is often a negative experience. We get psyched for the role, only to find out upon interviewing that there has been a lot of turnover and the comment is made that "we groom them for the next role they are looking for." Is this a valid, positive statement? Is this a team we want to be a leader on? As a leader we should be looking to build our staff for the long term. Worse yet, they are "selling you" on this leadership position. When you get the gut feeling that most of the conversation revolves around how great they are as a team, chances are they aren't.

Two different areas come through loud and clear when talking with prospective candidates: 1) They want to go to a team that will train and continue training, and 2) They know what team they want to go to because …

Whether starting a sales position or a leadership position, let's look at some of the options for the latter:

I only want to go to major league teams because if I don't start there, I'll never get there. Ask yourself: Am I just enamored with the thought of major leagues or do I truly want to work in sports? Minor league teams offer a tremendous potential to learn, grow AND move up to GM. They also give you the opportunity to prepare for that job at a major league team. Don't discount them. Most care about you and give you multiple opportunities to learn new things.

_____ is one of my favorite teams and I just have to work there. Teams don't hire fans, or they shouldn't. It's very hard to be objective when you're a fan. You can be a fan of the sport, but not a passionate fan of the team. I've known people who get into conversations with potential clients for an hour or more because they get more into the team, how they are playing, the acquisitions, etc, instead of the value of their purchase. There's a fine line between fandom and respect for a sport.

They're a winning team. I want to work there! Just my opinion, but some of the best teams you will work for are those on a losing streak. Why? In most highly successful teams, you are not selling but rather order-taking. It's easier to talk about the team, get them to agree, and ultimately sell. Working for a team with a less stellar record, you will be taught how to truly sell. NOW you are a salesperson.

POTATO CHIP LEADERSHIP SKILLS

In a leadership position, you are truly building strategy and process for success, which will make you invaluable in the future. Teams that are new and just starting can offer one of two things: either an order-taking position the first year or two, or truly having to sell it the first year or two. For the quick success teams, you will most likely not learn true sales or leadership until 3 years after that team is in place.

I want to learn, but I'm not sure how much training they will give me. So why not ask that? What is your training program? How often do you train? Do you bring in someone? Is it strictly in house? If you bring in people, do you bring in more than one throughout the year? Is it reinforced? As a leader in this position, will I be given the opportunity to continue my growth and learn how to better a strategic process, or be managed by numbers hit without being part of the process? Just like my daughter, what are you going to do to help me become the best I can be? I have had people go into inside sales positions where they started with a training, and then no training after and they were 6 months into it. This is not a one-and-done. You NEED training in inside sales, and it's a specific type of training. You need training no matter the level, from starting sales to Presidents of teams. This keeps the gray matter stimulated and challenged to try new things and keeps us from becoming complacent. We all need to keep learning.

We seem to do the same training all the time and I need something more. Ask for it. Define it. Whether moving on to a new team in sales or starting a leadership role, ask how they view training. Is it the same training year after year or is there a varying focus of development? What level of training will you be at? There is no one-size-fits-all: There is a basic level for inside sales, there is a mid-level for AEs, and then there is the All Star-type training that helps you be the best you can be, and also ready for that management spot you want. Once you get that management role, there should be management training. Where are they in trainings? Do they use all types depending on what level you are at? Do you fit with their philosophy on training?

Never stop learning. When you do, it's time to move on in your career. We all learn, each and every day. Start a journal. What did you learn today that helped you better communicate an idea, or close a sale, or ask better questions? Learn that one thing every day.

This is your career. Make sure you approach it that way. It should never be "I hope I get a job there," or "I hope I get this next leadership position" but rather, "I will take the steps to make sure I am making the right decisions and going to the team and culture that is best for me." It's work. It doesn't happen overnight. But it *will* happen with the right approach and the right mindset. And when it does, it will be a win for both you *and* the team.

POTATO CHIP LEADERSHIP SKILLS

OUR NEXT SALES LEADERS

In hiring the next sports sales leader, we tend to ask "leadership" questions about how they sold. This assumes, if they were a great seller, that they will transfer those tips to the team and the team will now be hugely successful. WRONG! It doesn't work that way. If nothing else, we have to remember that no two sales people are—or should be—alike. We are all unique. We can help guide, but we can't make mini-me's.

So, what is it we do ask? What is it we are looking for? The most overlooked area when hiring sports sales leaders is strategy. The "how." The process. The plan. Many teams, for lack of anything better, will ask for a 30/60/90-day plan. In all honesty, do you really think this leader is going to come in and help the team bring in $2 million in revenue in 90 days? They've just found the restroom, learned how to make coffee, finally got their business cards, learned the team's favorite watering hole, and had some basic questions answered after 30 days. So, what makes us think they'll have that big plan accomplished in 90 days?

What is most important is learning how the potential leader thinks through situations. What is their plan in these situations? This will help you know how much strategy they can grasp and how much help they might need. Every interview of potential leaders should include a strategy question. For example:

It's November. Please create your strategic plan based on the following expectations: Our season starts in April, here is where we expect our team to be:

- 100% in full season by the opener

- Fulfill 100% of our partial plans by June 15

- Groups need to be at 60% by the opener

- Hospitality needs to be 2/3 filled by May 1

- Corporate partnerships needs to be at 90% to goal by the opener

- Renewals to begin in July with a plan

- Focus seems to be the hardest for our sales team to grasp. Please share your strategy as to how you will help them focus by day yet still enjoy and contribute to the culture.

- Create a strategic plan for balance so that all areas are successful for a quarter.

- Create an offseason strategy for the first 3 months after the season ends so we can get ahead in sales.

- Two sales reps are low in numbers. What is your strategic plan to work with them to get them stronger?

There's so much more to this equation of leadership. A leader doesn't have to be the top seller. What they do need to be is someone who understands the process, can coach, and can create the strategy and put it in motion, thus guiding their team to success.

As their supervisor, what is YOUR strategic plan to grow them? What is the company's overall 3-year strategy and how can they best fulfill this? This is the type of thinking we need when hiring our next leader. It's not a case of put them in, wind them up, and hope they function. It's a case of moving the organization forward with the right people in place. It's great to see some of the young leaders out there who are moving their organizations forward. Nick Seckerson, Sr. Director at the El Paso Chihuahuas, is not a top-tier seller but rather a top-tier coach, motivator, and strategist. He not only thinks through and plans by month/quarter/year but he inspires and coaches his staff to do the same. Consequently, the team has a room full of potential leaders, as they themselves learn the process to be successful. Joe Isse, Director of Inside Sales with the Portland Trailblazers, is a strategic thinking coach. It's not a case of just hitting numbers for him; it's a case of preparing these young reps to be able to successfully take on a role as a full-time account executive. There is no better compliment than to hear his superiors say that they are so happy to move up one of his people because they are fully prepared for the next task at hand. These are strategic thinking leaders.

If your current leadership team is not focused on strategy yet, consider how much greater your organization could be if you help them improve in this process. As you look to hire, ask the hard questions. Look for those who not only can relate and coach but can also think strategically and help their team do the same.

POTATO CHIP LEADERSHIP SKILLS

BREAKING THE CYCLE

Job opportunities in the sports world increase seasonally. I get many questions from those in sales as to how to break through the barriers that seem to be set in place with so many teams. Granted, not everyone who applies for a position really fits the opportunity, but we as leaders interviewing and recruiters for positions need to look at more than what we have been narrowing jobs down to over the years. Our focus should be on looking at what this candidate has to offer and what it will take to set them up for success. Yes, we are looking at our needs, but also looking at how can we help this candidate start off on a positive note and be able to run with it. If we want them to be a change agent, can we let them do that and provide them the tools needed? Are we really okay with that?

I have seen so many teams have new employees join only to give them a book of "training" that is obsolete, uses scripts that are outdated (and why are we using them anyway?) and focused on call volume, and in no way gives them the ability to use their brain. I have seen teams hand out sheets that are from trainings from up to 15 years ago with scripts (!) that are useless. I have seen teams who have a 2-day onboarding process, after which you are expected to hit the ground running and sell well. Teams who want to bring you in as a change agent then just do the same thing that everyone else is doing. (I can see Einstein turning over in his grave right now!) Teams who make you jump through hoops as a candidate then ... crickets. I have to step back and ask if this is how we treat new employees, how are we dealing with the existing ones?

As we go through the process of hiring, here are a few things to think about:

Collaborate on recruiting: If a sales leader is not working in harmony with the HR leader, how will everyone be on the same page? Collaborate. Decide what is important in the sales position you are hiring for. Are you looking for someone like yourself (not the best move) or someone who will bring different strengths to the table and make an impact? Someone who will create some change and bring a different thought process?

Thoughts: Remember: you are only as good as the person you hire and train and invest in. Give your finalists the StrengthsFinder test. See where their top five lie and you'll know immediately which areas you will need to invest in them in so as to start them off for success. If you truly want someone to bring change to the organization, know that you will have to let go of the reigns and let them do this. Know through the recruiting process what their strategy is so you can accept it from the start.

Are there internal candidates being considered? Ask yourself the question: Am I doing all this interviewing to make sure I'm making the right decision (ie, am I that unsure of the internal candidate?) or am I doing it to make sure I fulfill our policy of open recruiting? Nothing is worse than stringing along external candidates when you know you are hiring internally.

Thoughts: I have seen so very often those who are unsure will bring an external candidate along to the final stage and then get cold feet. Not that the internal candidate was bad, but rather the leader feared change coming from an external candidate and the time it would take to invest in them. If you are looking to build the organization, change is inevitable. If you want to continue to do the same thing, you will have the same results, just with different people in place. Will you let the internal candidate create change or want them to continue to do what they are doing with a new title?

Dragging the process out. All too often, teams drag the process out. They have a finalist and then go AWOL. The reasons given: Maybe there's someone even better out there and we should keep looking, or worse, we don't want to really invest the money in them. Sales positions and leadership in sales positions are the most crucial investment you will make in the team—investment being the key word.

Thoughts: Pay for the talent, set the expectations, and then let them do their job. Dragging it out says two things to your staff: The position and hitting the goals aren't that important and we are not willing to invest in real talent. You have to have top talent on the court or field—to be successful off the court or field, you need to have that same top talent. You need to have coaches and trainers for both types of talent.

What if I make the wrong hiring decision? What if they don't work out? What if, what if, what if? If your expectations of the position are clear and you recognize that change is good and necessary, then look to find the best person you can to make it happen. Often, leadership hiring for the position is not truly clear on the expectations themselves, which leads to fear of making a "bad" decision.

Thoughts: Don't be afraid to ask for help in setting the expectations and the description of the job at hand. Will it be an important decision? Of course! When you buy a house or a car, do you not ask others for advice? This decision is every bit as important. Make sure you are clear as to what you are looking for and what your expectations will be by asking others.

Hiring someone to be a change agent then not letting them be one. You know the story. Your organization needs change. This person brings that change to the table. This is an area we can grow in (especially in B2B) and this is the person who can deliver. A few months into the job, you have them conform to the hundred calls a day, stick to the lists, and just produce. Not comfortable with change and not having immediate results while they build the relationships, you have them go to the "proven method that you were trying to break out of.

Thoughts: The greatest disservice we can do is bring people aboard to ask them to do what they do best, creating the change we want, and then, in fear of things not happening fast enough, asking them to conform to a method that has little use for brains, creativity, or passion. And we get upset when they leave. If we believe in them enough to bring them aboard to create the change, we have to give them at least 6 months to build the culture and the relationships needed so they can make that change happen. Expecting immediate results with a method new to the company is like putting your house up for sale with a realtor and firing them after the first 3 days because it isn't sold. Let them follow their process and go along with them on their journey, checking in and holding them accountable, but letting them use their talent and skills to get them to success.

Inside sales positions: This is often a "make or break" role for those stepping into the sports world. It is not, as it used to be, the doorway into sports. It is a sales position, and one in which your goal should be to grow. Are we hiring correctly and preparing them correctly? Are we looking to truly use this as a growth and development opportunity or rather to fill quotas and sell our inventory with minimal investment in their growth? Define your program.

Thoughts: No question, inside sales programs bring aboard additional sales. The key is that they are immediate sales and not necessarily for the long term, as most programs do not build relationships but rather dial for dollars. A true inside sales program should be a Sales Growth and Development Program. Teach them important tools for career growth: how to prospect without a lead list, how to set appointments, how to go to a client's workplace and meet with them, how to influence, how to execute, how to build a strategic sales plan, how to build a sustainable relationship so that what is being sold to them will not be dropped the following year.

Bringing in a new leadership person. What is the training process? Am I going to give them the reigns or hold on tightly? Am I looking for someone to sell, lead, and take over whatever areas need help? Or am I looking to grow and develop a leader who will cultivate the staff and hit goals?

Thoughts: Leadership roles are opportunity roles. Without investment, we set them up for failure. Have your investment plan in place before hiring.

I have had the pleasure of talking with teams who are in the process of hiring and know exactly what the position entails, the expectations, the type of person they are looking for to assist with culture/strengths, etc, and are open to change. These are teams who are not filling slots but are actually growing their business with people who will bring new ideas to the table. At the end of the day, our job as leaders is very similar to that of being a parent: grow them, develop them, give them the opportunity to gain the tools to be successful, then give them wings. A team's job is to give them the opportunity with a clear and concise onboarding and structure so that they will be able to succeed and give you the results you want. When a potential hire is taken to that last step and then hears nothing, you are in essence showing them the type of organization they just may be working for.

We need to build better relationships with our applicants to show that we, as a business, are in the business of building relationships. Once hired, we need to believe in them and let them be the change agents we hired them to be. This is the best opportunity we have to break the cycle of how/why we hire and prove to Einstein that we are not afraid to make the change!

THE FIFTH CHIP

ONBOARDING

Whether leader or sales associate, a strong onboarding process is key to success. Teams who onboard for a day or two and then have employees hit the phones or start leading are setting the new hire up for failure as well as creating cultural hurricanes. The most important part of the hiring process is the onboarding process. This shows a new hire that we wanted them, we prepared for them, and we are investing in them from day one. How many times did you start a new position only to wait for business cards for a month or more? Or your computer isn't set up for a week? No pens? No post-its? Really looks like they wanted you, right?

A strong onboarding process in sales will include preparation before their start date, meeting the departments, understanding how to work together, learning the ticketing system, and having hands-on experience with it.

It includes sample calls and not going "live" until everyone feels comfortable. It means understanding and utilizing CRM.

A strong leadership onboarding will include in-depth evaluations of employees and learning a patient process to change. I'm a huge fan of a minimum 2-week onboarding process. Anything less is hiring a body.

A SAMPLE NEW SALES EMPLOYEE ONBOARDING

How the new sales employee should be viewed:

This is prime time for the new employee to feel they made the right decision coming aboard.

- It takes 3 months to build relationships; no great sales expectations should be made during that time … the most important part of the 3 months is building the background, the client pipeline, and learning to call/meet successfully.

- Are you prepared for them to start?

- Nothing is more appreciated when starting a job than feeling that you are wanted: pens, notepads, post-its, a stapler, tape, and business cards are on your desk. Computer is turned on and ready. A welcome to your new home card signed by the staff is an amazing feeling.

- This should be on any new employee's onboarding checklist prior to their starting.

Purpose of onboarding:

- Communication! Can't say it enough … our teams are failing because of poor communication or insufficient communication. The best thing you can do in onboarding is communicating clearly to them *and most importantly having them repeat back to you so that you know that they heard what you think you said.* Give them time to understand the business.

- An opportunity to learn about their leaders so they can best determine how to manage up.

- The opportunity to start to learn processes.

- Most importantly, it shows you **value** them … you value them enough to spend time with them, not expecting them to jump right in, and you are **prepared** for them.

Suggested onboarding process:

- Suggest a minimum 2- to 3-week onboarding process with a 3- to 6-month development plan; once our new rep starts making practice calls, when Sr. Manager feels they are ready to call they should have the VP or President be called for the final check-off.

- Week 1 should focus on learning about each department and their processes and systems.

- Week 2 should focus on getting to know the staff and starting to practice calls, practice the ticketing system you are using, practice CRM, and be signed off on all before going live.

- If not signed off in 2 weeks, continue practice calls until signed off.

Overall, let them know how much they are empowered so they are able to have "tools in their toolbox" and can make decisions without having to ask each time.

ONBOARDING WEEK ONE: Focus on Learning

MONDAY

9-10 Meet with President and VP

- Welcome

- Philosophy overview

- Where you see their role in this process

- Why exactly did you bring them aboard?

- What do you feel they can bring to the organization?

11-12 Meet with Director or Sr. Manager. This should be a walkthrough of the offices with introductions to all staff. This is simply an intro meeting. Director or Sr. Manager should be prepared to say something positive about each person you introduce them to as to their strength in the organization.

12-1:30 Lunch. This should be an all-department staff lunch. Everyone should go somewhere together, relax, and welcome the new hire.

1:30-2:30 Meet with the VP again

- Bit of a history of the organization

- Your expectations clearly communicated as to how you envision his/her role and how you arrive at goal setting

2:30-4   Meeting Director/Sr. Manager

- Clear communication of the role

- Coaching. Explain the coaching plan you will use

- Motivation. How does he/she get motivated? What sparks their interest?

- Communicating clearly with teammates. Make sure everyone is on the same page.

- Explain the usage of whiteboards.

- Explain the process of a person buying season tickets from start till the upcoming year; groups; premium so that they see and understand you are process oriented.

- Explain the product. Encourage ideas as to how to best introduce people to our product.

4-5 Intro and HR paperwork

TUESDAY

Focus of learning will be ticketing operations: have the department plan to have new hire aboard the whole day.

Meet with Ticket Ops Director at 9

- Review the process of a sale (season/group/premium) on the ticketing system

- How do they assist sales?

- Seating charts: explain pricing structure

- CRM and info input into the system: why it's necessary; the value it can bring

- Analytics: how/what do they draw

- Review everyone's role in this department

- Come back with an understanding of how sales and ticket ops currently work and how the processes work

- Remainder of day: review ticketing system on computer; practice with input, building in a client, etc. Have someone from ticket ops work 1:1 with new hire

- Check in during the last half hour with Director/Sr. Manager.

WEDNESDAY

Focus of learning will be Marketing/Communication.

Meet with Marketing Director at 9

- Listen and learn their philosophy on the marketing of the product

- How do they assist sales?

- Review the process with them

- Learn the social media side of marketing and understand and learn how sales can best benefit or add to this

- Review past marketing pieces

Goal: come back with an understanding of sales and marketing and how marketing can assist with individual social media sales

Remainder of day: Review accounts on ticketing system; learn how to look for things on ticketing system; review CRM notes; understand the input you will need to make

Review marketing pieces for the past events

Last half hour: check in with VP and update so far

THURSDAY

Focus of learning is the facility and its functions.

Meet with Guest Services director at 9

- Listen and learn their philosophy on servicing the clients

- How does this assist sales?

- Review the process with them

- Understand how problems get solved; the process and chain of command

- How do client problems get discussed afterwards with staff so as to prevent future problems?

- Walk the new hire through the event day in guest services

- Have GS director and a sales rep take them around, explaining each area and pros and cons

Goal: come back with an understanding of how sales can best work with and communicate with guest services and a better understanding of areas to sell, as well as ideas of different uses for areas

Remainder of day: Review premium areas accounts in ticketing system; look for patterns of who buys/types; review different areas and look for patterns. Review guest service issues over the past few year (if there is a log kept) and understand how they can be eliminated through the sales process

Last half hour: check in with Director/Sr. Manager

FRIDAY

Focus: Premium and Corporate. Meet with Corporate Partners Leadership at 9

Understand their process

- How does a sales staff member contribute?

- What constitutes a corporate client? What are the needs-based questions that are generally asked?

- Goal: gain an understanding of how we can best help each other in increasing sales

- Meet with Premium Leadership at 10:30

- Understand their process

- Understanding the who/how of a premium sale

- Prospecting process

- What constitutes a premium client?

- Steps to a premium sale; follow up once made

- Steps week prior with the premium sale

- The premium checklist

- What are the types of complaints one hears from premium clients; how do we address them?

Goal: understand the how/why/who of who is currently being sought after and sold to in premium; review the process to both prospecting and the sale

Remainder of the day: work on your personal business strategy for the upcoming 30 days

Last half hour: meet with Director/Sr. Manager

ONBOARDING WEEK 2: Getting to Know the "Nuts and Bolts"

MONDAY

9-11 Meet with sales buddy

- Have them explain their sales process

- How do they prospect

- How do they network

- How many in person meetings do they have a week

- Sales tips

1-5 Learn

- Listen in on sales members calls for 2 hours

- Last 2 hours, role play with different sales staff members on calls

- Role play with 2 different sales members by using phone and calling them; critique afterwards and get pointers

TUESDAY

9-9:30   Meet with sales buddy

- Review sales calls day prior

- Get pointers

9:30-10:30 Observe calls with follow up CRM notes

POTATO CHIP LEADERSHIP SKILLS

Listen in and input into CRM for the reps or input after the call

10:30-12 Practice sessions (created by Director or Sr. Manager) in ticketing system

- Worksheet to find things in specific accounts

- Worksheet to find seating and payments on select accounts

- Inputting 3 new sales into the system (season, group and premium)

- Needs to be signed off on this so practice sessions need to be built in to the schedule until mastered

Lunch

1-2 Prospecting for clients: who are our people, where will I find them, start to research, and build pipeline

2-3:30 Practice calls to reps for season/group (assign reps); critique after

3:30-4:30 Practice sessions on CRM or ticketing system as needed

WEDNESDAY

9-9:30 Meet with sales buddy

9:30-11 Practice call sessions with sales reps and box office reps

11-12 Work on building pipeline; prospecting

Lunch

1-2:30 Meet with Director/Sr. Manager: role play in person meetings; call to Director/Sr. Manager and have reviewed

2:30-4:30 Practice calls with "purchases" and input into the system

THURSDAY

9-9:30 Meet with sales buddy

9:30-12:00 Practice calls to Financial Planners (arrange with corporate partners) with critique after each

Lunch

1-2:30 Prospecting for pipeline

2:30-4 Practice calls last run with 'purchase' and input into system

4:00-4:30 Meet with Director /Sr. Mgr.

FRIDAY

9-9:30 Meet with sales buddy

9:30-12:00 If practice calls have gone well, practice calls to Sr. management (VP, President)

Sign off on these calls if you feel they are good enough to go live

Lunch

1:00-3:00 If approved, go live with prospect list started

3:00-5:00 Prospect more for pipeline

ONBOARDING LEADERS

How the new leaders should be viewed:

- If they were hired just prior to the season starting, it is extremely important that these weeks leading up to the opener are not considered do or die or "add-on numbers" for the new managers.

- The only leaders who are successful are those who ease in and gain trust. This is crucial.

- If you feel you need to give them a sales goal, make it extremely nominal ... extremely. Why? Your management team should have one purpose: to coach their team to hit their goals. Control what they can control. They can't control numbers but they can control the coaching of your people so that your team hits their goals. If you have the management team divided partly into focusing on the team and partly to hitting their own sales goals, nine times out of ten the stress of hitting the goals takes over and they are not doing what you hired them for ... coaching their team.

Are you prepared for them to start?

- In addition to the business cards, the computer, and so on, start out with a welcome to the team.

- What's been our record? A look at the department over the past 3-5 years should be printed out and on their desk. They need to know where it's been to understand where it's going.

- Who are the players? Also included should be a short bio on each rep they will be leading. Where they are from, length of time there, revenue goals each year they've been there, and where they personally ended.

- How do we currently play the game? Give them a single sheet on how their staff runs on a typical day. If there is a power hour at 8:30, list it and say where it occurs. They need to have a feel right from the start of how their team functions.

- What is our schedule? Give them a printed schedule for the next couple of weeks so they know exactly where they will be and when and who they are meeting.

Purpose of leadership onboarding:

Communication

Goal: Understand current communication process. Assess. See if it is working well with your team. Make notes to observe further

Observation

Goal: Make a list of habits that could be better, better time management, needs in the sales process, observing each rep and understanding their sales style or leadership style and if it is working for them.

Assessment

- What are the methods your team uses to measure success? What are the methods they use to plan for their day?

Understanding

- Where has the team been? Where is it going? What will you be able to contribute?

Comprehensive review

- Reviewing all historical data available and understanding the direction of the staff previously. What have been the results? What were the circumstances surrounding it?

Learning processes already in place

- What is the process used by those who report to you? Is it well thought out? Can it be stronger? What are the steps to a better process that you would recommend? Make note of this.

- Learning "managing up" processes as well as lateral managing processes

- Get to know your supervisor. How do they best like to communicate? Are they overwhelmed? What can you do in your role that would make them more efficient in their role? Lateral: What is the communication method best used between leaders of other departments? What is the follow-up process? How do they most like to receive suggestions?

Suggested onboarding process:

1. Suggest a minimum 2-week to 3-month onboarding process

ONBOARDING WEEK ONE: *Focus on Meeting the Team*

Example: Director position

MONDAY

9-11 President

- Welcome

- Philosophy overview

- Review visionary process (let them know that the 3- to 5-year plan is evolving and they will be part of the planning process)

- Walk them through where the organization was and what ownership believes needs to be changed

- Where they see your role in this process

- Why exactly were they brought aboard?

- What do you feel they can bring to the organization?

- Give an overview on how as leaders you are growing and changing mindset of the way things have been done, such as working to include staff more and create a more collaborative and passionate culture

- Understanding of goals of past year and what the results were

11-12   Meeting #1 with VP. This should be a walkthrough of the offices, with introductions to all staff. This is simply an intro meeting. VP should be prepared to say something positive about each person you introduce him or her to as to their strength in the organization.

12-1:30 Lunch. This should be your team and your VP with you. Everyone should go somewhere together and have casual conversation.

1:30-2:30 Meeting with the PR or Communications VP

- History of the organization and the area it encompasses

- How the team name evolved, fan base, etc.

2:30-4:00 Meeting #2 With VP

- Clear communication of role

- Coaching. What are the expectations of coaching meetings with team? What has been done currently and what were the results?

- Motivation. What are the expectations for contests, positive culture, etc? What has been done currently and what have been the results?

- Communicating clearly with their staff. Processes currently used to communicate and is it working?

- Whiteboards. Usage currently and has it been motivational, helpful or just another thing?

- Learn current processes and be prepared to make recommendations to streamline for upcoming year.

- Work with VP on creating new processes for success and for our clients so that they see and feel the value of being a member of the organization.

- Active, coaching leader but what does this mean? Communicate, communicate, communicate.

- Do a department breakdown. Explain where everyone fits right now, with the understanding we may be changing the org chart.

- Explain where each person is in regards to goal right now and what you have observed as some of the challenges.

4-5 HR paperwork

TUESDAY

Focus of learning will be ticketing system: have ticketing plan to have leader aboard the whole day

Meet with Ticket Ops Director at 9

- Listen and learn how they have done renewals and why

- Review the process with them

- How do they assist sales?

- Review the process of a sale: point of sale to input in the system to printing of the tickets

- Seating charts

- Analytics: how/what do they draw?

- Review everyone's role in this department

- Meet all the staff and have a few minutes to talk with each of them

- Come back with an understanding of how Sales and Ticket Ops currently work and how the processes could work better for the good of the organization and the sales process

- Learn the system if not familiar: have someone from Ticket Ops work one on one with new Director

Remainder of day: If not familiar with the system, review ticketing system on computer; practice with input, building in a client, etc.

Check in last half hour with VP for review

WEDNESDAY

- Focus of learning will be Marketing/Communications

- Meet with Marketing Director at 9

- Listen and learn their philosophy on the marketing strategy

- How do they assist sales?

- Review the process with them

- Learn the social media side of marketing and understand and learn how sales can best benefit or add to this

- What is the % of following on each social media site?

- How do they currently present season, group, hospitality options on social media?

- What are their strongest demographics? Who are they trying to capture?

- Review past marketing pieces

- How can we better relate our sales staff to marketing?

Goal: Come back with an understanding of how sales can best work with marketing so every marketing piece has a sales message somehow and how marketing can assist each rep with individual social media sales

Remainder of day

Review accounts on ticketing system for each rep; review CRM notes; understand how we can get better in these areas

Review marketing pieces for the past year and the results of each; understand what worked/didn't and try to learn why

Last half hour: Check in with VP

THURSDAY

- Focus is on learning the facility and its functions

Meet with Guest Services Director at 9

- Listen and learn their philosophy on servicing the clients

- How does this assist sales?

- Review the process with them

- Understand how problems get solved; the process and chain of command

- How do client problems get discussed after with staff so as to prevent for the future?

- Walk the new Director through the event day in Guest Services

- Have Guest Services Director and a Sales rep take them around, explaining each area and its pros and cons

Goal: Come back with an understanding of how Sales can best work and communicate with Guest Services and a better understanding of areas to sell, as well as ideas of different uses for areas

Remainder of day:

Review premium areas accounts in ticketing system; look for patterns of who buys/ types; review different areas and look for patterns

Review guest service issues over the past season (if there is a log kept) and understand how they can be eliminated through the sales process

Last half hour: Check in with the VP

FRIDAY

Meet with CP at 9

- Understand their process

- How does the sales staff contribute? What is the relationship between the sales staff and corporate? How does corporate contribute to group and season and premium?

- What constitutes a corporate client? What are the needs based questions that are generally asked?

Goal: Gain an understanding of how we can best help each other in increasing sales

Meet with Premium at 10:30

- Understand their process

- Understanding the who/how of a premium sale with this product

- Prospecting process

- What constitutes a premium client?

- Steps to a premium sale; follow up once made

- Steps week prior with the premium sale

- Is there a premium checklist?

- Could one be created?

- What are the types of complaints one hears from premium clients; how do we address them?

Goal: Understand the how/why/who of who is currently being sought after and sold to in premium; review the process to both prospecting and the sale and are there ways to streamline; ideas for creating a checklist for premium to facilitate the process of the sale, the days prior to the event, and the event itself

Remainder of the day: Start to create notes that the new Director will share later as to how departments can best work together efficiently and also start to create a strategy for the premium process; start to think through a premium checklist and work with the premium leader on creating that

Last half hour: Meet with VP

ONBOARDING WEEK 2: *Getting to Know the Staff*

Monday, Tuesday, Wednesday, Thursday, Friday

2 Individual meetings in the morning: one at 9, one at 10:30

- Have them explain their sales process

- How do they prospect?

- How do they network?

- How many in-person meetings do they have a week?

- Ask how they best learn

- Ask how they feel about meetings: too many, too few, is communication good?

POTATO CHIP LEADERSHIP SKILLS

Explain to them: If I were to create a coaching plan for you, what areas would you think I should focus on with you?

- What is the hardest part of the job? The easiest? What is their favorite sale?

- Get to know them outside the office: What are their hobbies, what are their outside interests? Is there something they have as a goal they are working on outside of the office?

Afternoons:

- Review the sales records of the 2 reps met with

- Review the strengths chart: What areas are they lacking in the top 5 (any category)? How can we best create a plan that will help them?

- General observations after the 1:1s: how can you best support them, basic assessment, notes to continue to watch for so you can create your coaching plan

- Start to create the coaching plan for each

- Prior to leaving each day: discuss with VP

Also this week:

- Thought process for whiteboards for Sales

- Strategy as to what would be most efficient for the upcoming year and would help facilitate sales, as well as create an easier focus

- Communication and buzz in the sales room

- Is it there, is it lacking, what can be done?

- Suggestions for prospecting ideas and how you can best support them

- What type of workshops can you create to help with prospecting?

- Create your plan as to how you feel you will best coach this team to success and the how of sales meetings, etc.

- How can we create the energy/process/contest? For a sale a day … starting new habits

Potato Chip Trainers

Parameters

- Identify your current parameters for hiring (college, experience, etc)

- Looking at the list, write the qualifications you desire based on the experience or molding you want. What is different from the first list?

Questions

- Look at your existing team. What qualities need strengthening?

- Create five questions that pertain to those qualities. Use those in interviewing.

- Add these qualities needed to your job description for this particular position.

Who do you hire?

- Create five questions that get them to discuss past experiences and how they handled situations as well as why they want to sell.

- Add these to your job description with the walks of life you are willing to interview.

Create a hiring strategy

- Define the candidate you are looking for. In sales, we create a sales strategy. In hiring, we should also be creating a hiring strategy.

- Create one or two strategy questions for them to put together and either send back to you as part of the interview process or ask them during the interview process.

- Create a timeline for hiring

- When hiring, create a timeline for accepting candidates, interviewing first round, final round, and decision.

- Be able to define when the candidate will come aboard full time should the correct candidate be found.

Onboarding

Start the outline for an onboarding process for a new leader or a sales associate remembering they will only be as good as the time you invest in them. Have a template ready.

The Sixth
Potato Chip

EVALUATING YOUR TEAM

One of the most dreaded exercises I hear about from leaders is writing the yearly evaluations. Never sure what to say, how to say it, how to present it, fear of getting an employee upset, and retaliation all go through a leader's mind.

Think about the flip side. What goes through the mind of the sales rep? "Are they going to be fair? How will this affect my pay? If it's a numbering system, how do they number?"

There is nothing worse than evaluations being dreaded by both the giver and receiver. As a leader, you receive your evaluation from your supervisor. As a supervisor, the evaluation should be focused on the growth of both the team and the leader, not strictly did they or did they not hit numbers. Has the team shown improvement? Is the team energized? Are they creating plans and going after them? Are they creating relationships and establishing solid pipelines? This is all attributed to the leader. Has the leader shown growth? Are they able to build a strategic plan with the team? Are they creating and being responsible for attaining goals? Are they able to be counted on instead of repeatedly asked? These are things that show growth as a leader.

Why do we do evaluations? Many think it's because it's the busy work of an HR department. (Sorry HR!) In reality, it gives us the opportunity to coach our people to next steps. If done correctly, it can be a very positive motivator. If done as a chore, it will come across that way and end up being a demotivator.

Information in evaluations should never be a surprise if we have been doing our job all along as leaders. If we have been coaching one on one throughout the year, then this is actually a summarization of growth. There are no surprises then. Everyone should know where they stand all along and measurably how they can grow so they *can* grow, versus coming in one day at an evaluation and being given a list of deficiencies. Teams in which leaders view their 1:1 coaching as "what's in your pipeline?" and whether "you're making seventy calls?" are hurting their employees in the long run, as they are not growing them, rather they are setting their employee up for frustration (as well as their leader) in having to go through the evaluation process with unknowns. Unfortunately, I have had many leaders tell me they don't keep good notes throughout the year and, when doing evaluations, they look at the last month and rate them on that. This is so sad on so many levels. Again, go back to your coaching sessions. Keep a record. Make them count.

When to do them? As I mentioned, if done yearly or twice yearly, they should truly be a summarization of all of the coaching sessions showing the growth. Actually, every 1:1 coaching session is a mini-evaluation. Let's look at what you have, where you are going, point out an area to grow in, and give some steps to take to grow— you now have a small-scale evaluation. Create your coaching sheet, put it in their file, and there really is no need for a formal evaluation. All the information HR or anyone needs is part of the 1:1s.

Is it logical to tie bonuses and raises to evaluations? In my years of both working and consulting, I have seen more demotivation from this than anything. If there is a cost of living raise, why is it done at the evaluation? If a bonus or raise is earned throughout the year, why not call the rep in and give it to them? Isn't this more of a motivating factor than to wait till the end of the year to see what you might or might not be paid? If I spend 3 months working on a project that increased my sales by a considerable amount, is that not worth a bonus right then? If over 6 months I consistently raise my revenue, is it not motivating to offer me a bump in pay for my focus and work? Does it not make me want to do it even more the next 6 months? Performance raises given after a great performance can bolster a sales rep's confidence and build great culture.

If we keep a copy of each week's coaching sheets and summarize at the end of each month the growth pattern of our reps, evaluations will no longer be dreaded but rather a monthly summarization of growth. Measurable suggestions for further growth are the perfect way to end the evaluation.

TYPES OF EVALUATIONS

Although there are at least six different styles of evaluations, the two most commonly used are the numbering system and the written system. A third is the combination of the two.

Many teams use a numbering system, feeling it is easier and more objective and gives a department a number an employee has to reach to be considered for other levels. What are the pros and cons of a numbering system for evaluations?

Pros:

- They're easier.

- You can add up the numbers and create a spot to put each employee.

- Theoretically, they are objective.

Cons:

- The rep is at the mercy of a leader who, although trained in the system, often relies on what they feel is right in numbering. For example, I've had leaders who have believed on a 1 to 5 scale, no one should ever be above a 4 and most should be at a 2 or 3. Meanwhile, other leaders give their reps 4s and 5s.

- Tends to be more subjective, based on numbers not on specifics.

- A very demotivating system in most teams and businesses and tends to breed turnover.

The second type of evaluation is the written one. A little more time consuming, it takes more thought yet can be very objective if done correctly.

Pros:

- Does not assign a number to a person but rather gives insight into where they have grown and where they need to grow.

- More of an interactive review and, if written correctly, can give the rep the opportunity to continue growth in a positive way.

- Gives measurable examples.

- Can be easily done if based off of strong coaching sessions done weekly or biweekly.

Cons:

- Tedious for leaders who do not do coaching sessions or do not do them correctly.

- For some leaders, this becomes a negative instead of a positive, pointing out all the problems and negative sides. In reality, this should not come up at all if the leader has been doing coaching sessions all along. The only time a negative comment would come up is if the growth has not been shown during the coaching sessions or improvement has not been made.

- If not coaching all along, it will not be an interactive review but rather a judgmental review.

So how will you as a leader handle a review? What are the steps to a strong evaluation?

There are three steps:

Are the objectives clear, understood, and measurable? As leaders, we should never create vague or misinterpreted evaluations. They should not be opinions but rather based on fact and can be measured. If someone has been coached about being late and continues to be late, we need to say, "John has a pattern of starting work late that has not been improving upon coaching. Even though coached each month on this, John was late 5 times in October, 4 times in November and 6 times in December. The tardiness ranges from 5 minutes to 20 minutes." This is concrete. This is measurable. This is clear. It is not an emotional statement but rather one of fact.

Document results throughout the year. This gives you objective information rather than subjective.

Provide consistent feedback throughout the year and chart growth. This enables you to have less angst presenting and the rep is more receptive to receiving. There are no surprises. You are stating where the rep needed to grow, the steps they took to grow, and if they accomplished growth.

Evaluations can make or break our reps, especially our younger ones who are still trying to figure us out as leaders. Bring them along on the journey instead of setting them up for potential target practice. Work with them throughout the year. Consider quarterly evaluations, which give them the opportunity to see growth more easily. This can be tied into their quarterly strategies. The consistency of growth will be much stronger and the evaluation so often dreaded by both leader and rep will no longer be a sore spot.

POTATO CHIP LEADERSHIP SKILLS

THE GOOD, THE BAD & WHY BOTHER?

Somewhere for some reason, a leader decided they didn't want to do evaluations anymore and, in the spirit of "ownership," they started asking their reps to do their own evaluations, after which they would just weigh in and sign off.

I haven't stopped scratching my head on that one. It's bad enough that as leaders we evaluate then ask the rep to evaluate to see if we are close.

But to turn it over entirely to the rep and sign off if we agree—that to me is … well, insulting. It tells me you don't know me well enough or my work.

It tells me I am not that important. It tells me you don't have the time to invest in us or coach us.

What are some "what not to do's" as leaders in evaluations?

- Don't make the rep do their own, especially for the reasons stated above.

- Don't raise issues without examples. Have concrete examples of when it happened and how it happened rather than speaking in generalities.

- Don't discuss personalities. Focus on behavior not on the person.

- Don't focus on the near term. If the evaluation is over a year, look at the growth or lack thereof throughout the whole year, not the last few weeks in which you wrote it.

- Don't compare. Nothing worse in an evaluation than comparing your rep to another rep in the room. Great way to destroy any remaining culture.

- Don't make promises. You say, "Maybe," and the rep hears, "Definitely." Don't even bring up a suggestion of a promise. You say, "We might have an opening in that department in the spring," and the rep hears, "There's going to be an opening in that department in the spring and they're going to put me in it."

- Don't ignore the previous review. They should be showing growth or lack thereof. Make sure the rep has both so they can follow along with your logic of growth or regression.

What are some to-dos as a leader?

- Give specific targeted goals for them to accomplish that will continue their growth. I would generally say, "To continue to grow, here are two things John should work on over the next 3 months …" Whatever you write, make sure it is something that can be measurable.

- Give them specific dates to hit goals by.

- Give positives as well as negatives.

- Create realistic goals. Sometimes leaders use an evaluation to have someone leave, without having the courage to release them. In so doing, they create highly unrealistic goals. In essence, you are deliberately setting them up to fail.

- Focus on performance not personality.

- Ask for their comments. Discuss them. Note them.

- Leave on a positive note. There is nothing worse than ending on a negative note, then having the rep go out and try to function for the rest of the day.

Evaluations can be one of the most constructive methods for growth if we manage them correctly. Don't leave them till the last minute, be coaching all along, use the highlights of the coaching, and use the evaluation for what it is meant for: a review of their growth/regression/development for the past ___ months.

COACHING SESSION EXAMPLE

Name:

Title:

Review of past two weeks:

Expectations for next two weeks:

Discuss growth goals that should be achieved in the upcoming months. Select the 2 that are most important to focus on right now for the next week or two that you both agree on.

What would these growth goals look like? If new sales, either deposits or paid in full. If in person meetings, then a recap written of the meeting with next steps. What is the follow up? If learning to use influencing more strongly, then list ways to influence in conversation and set a goal to use at least one in every conversation, etc. If prospecting needs to improve, then help show them ways to prospect and have them build it into their day and have a sheet ready for power hours each night before they leave.

Can be as simple as setting meetings: 20 calls per week with a goal of setting 5 meetings from those calls.

Invitation:

Together, decide what the weekly growth goals will be. Decide together how they will be achieved? Who will they go after? How? What is the focus? What can they do differently each day to achieve this? What is their pipeline? How can they improve it? What pipeline is needed to hit the goals for this month?

Discuss with them what this does for them as to achieving goals and where it fits in to the overall organizational revenue. Why is it important?

How will we measure progress?

Ask them how they will view progress each week. What will they need to report back on their 1:1 each week? What will they need to show they are achieving the growth goal?

Example: who have they met with, what was the convo, what is holding back a commitment, what can we do to move the commitment forward, opt to attend random meetings with them

Providing Feedback:

Example: we will continue to meet every other week, will measure success with your growth goals, offer suggestions and help, and measure how the growth goals have helped you

Will you be able to achieve? If not, what help do you need? What is holding your support up?

Evaluate Effectiveness:

At end of month: Monthly note

Growth goals achieved? ___yes ___ no

What worked?

What didn't work?

What could be better?

How did they show improvement? New skill(s) gained?

Biweekly: continue coaching forms and add one or two measurable growth goals

Following Month: repeat monthly form

Measuring progress will include keeping up with first 2

Potato Chip Trainers

Take a look at past evaluations you have done or have had done to you. What has been measurable? What was subjective? How can you change the pattern?

If using the numbering system, understand what each number should represent. Make sure that is conveyed to both your supervisor and to the reps. Be consistent in your evaluating by having consistency in the rationale for the numbers.

Create a checklist of to-dos to create great evaluations. Check it off after writing each. Did you accomplish the correct objectives?

Create and use weekly/biweekly coaching sheets as the key for the evaluations. Summarize on a monthly form to pull for the evaluations.

The Seventh
Potato Chip

SIX STEPS TO FILLING YOUR TEAM'S BENCH SUCCESSFULLY

I have had many requests from sports leaders as to what it would take to have their staff feel a more vested part of the business side of the organization. It has led to interesting conversations and many different styles of leadership. There have been contests (always fun), sales boards, trainings. The fact is, people want to be valued, they want to show they are worth something and they want to be appreciated for their contributions. Most importantly, they want to understand the organization, what the future strategy is for the organization, and where they fit into fulfilling that strategy each year, thus understanding their value to the organization. They really do want to use their brain and feel they are making an impact. There are teams who have achieved this and have successful, motivated sales teams … teams who are excited to come to work every day. How to get there?

Here are six steps I suggest to begin with to get your staff more engaged on the business side for the long term:

1. **Empowerment.**

Big word, great in theory, but often forgotten when it comes to use. We want it done *our* way. We want them to create more sales but only by *our* model. We encourage them to take care of our customers but only in *our* way. This is robotic … not empowerment.

Never forget the cardinal rule: the best ideas come from the people "in the trenches" … those who are out there selling every day. They hear the customers' needs, wants, frustrations, and emotions. If you want ideas, ask them then listen to them.

One of the biggest keys you will find to engagement: empower them to create their own sales ideas—different ways to sell, unique group ideas, unique ways to sell season or premium. Empower them to have tools in their toolkit to make a decision with the client at the moment. Encourage them to come up with off the wall corporate sponsorships that may very well end up raising a lot of revenue.

Don't be afraid to let them try. I promise you one thing: they will put all their energy and time into making it successful. Why? Because it was *their* idea. **No one wants their own idea to fail.** Look at your own ideas as a leader … don't we tend to tell our staff this is what we want because we don't want OUR ideas to fail? Empower them to do that same thing … check in with them, see how it is going. Give praise if it'sgoing well, offer guidance if it isn't. How can they grow if we don't let them use their gray matter?

1.   Business Strategy: Engagement

Prior to each quarter, each member of your staff should write their Personal Business Strategy. This helps them learn how to run their own small business. They need to review the past year's ups and downs both personally and on the field/floor, to their strengths, to what worked/didn't, to what is their detailed plan to make this quarter better than last year's quarter (this strategy is outlined in my first book, *Potato Chip Ticket Sales.*) What will be the challenges and how do they plan to overcome them? Let them decide how and when they will bring in the revenue for that quarter's goal, how much do they plan during each week of that quarter, etc. How much revenue will they bring in per month/week/day? Have them analyze it and plan it out. The point is, they are learning to view their work as their own small business. Breaking it down holds them accountable. And when you set the how, when, and who yourself, **you don't want it to fail and you have more buy-in**. When you have your weekly or biweekly coaching meetings, you have a quarterly plan to work with. No surprises on their part, a deeper understanding of the strategic process, and they will feel more in control of their sales.

Engage them in the company's 3- to 5-year strategic plan. This should be a meeting right after each season. Where is the company going in the next 3 to 5 years? Now let's look at year one and how the contributions you make will lead us to the growth we are looking to bring.

2.   Unleashing What They Do Best: Cater to Strengths

Everyone has their top five strengths. Managing those strengths to their advantage in sales does two things: helps them achieve their sales numbers and provides a **positive motivating factor in their daily work**. Do you know each team member's top five strengths? Do you help them find ways to best use them in sales?

3. Use "Grind" In A Positive Way: Work Hard, Play Hard

You are in it together. Achieve goals, play hard. Achieve more goals, play hard again. Yes, to sell is your job. But there is no law that says there can't actually be some fun to the hard side of selling! Make sure that contests are team contests. Individual contests may seem fun and be a driver to some, but if someone takes off and runs with it, the others feel they don't have a chance and it actually demotivates. Set goals, celebrate successes. The product on the field/court/ice plays as a team and celebrates successes as a team. As should we.

4. Celebrate Wins: Awards Ceremony

Be a believer in an end-of-the-year awards ceremony. Sports is not a 9 to 5 job, as we all know. Many of our reps have families/significant others who they don't see as much as they would like. The key to a successful awards ceremony is to invite their significant other. I've generally done the ceremony as an Academy Awards Ceremony, complete with red carpet and paparazzi. Include dinner. Have awards of all types: Rookie of the Year (over all departments), third, second, first place for each category, Highest Revenue Generator for groups/season/premium/corporate, Most Improved, Largest Single Sale for each department, the department who exceeded goals, etc, etc, etc. **It's a great feeling to be awarded in front of your peers and family.** And most importantly, if you weren't the one getting the award this year, you don't want to be the one left out next year. That competitive spirit kicks in. This is a motivator. It's amazing to be recognized by the executives of the organization. Have a player still in town? Ask them to attend and be master of ceremonies.

5. Where It Starts … YOU

You are the biggest catalyst to engagement. You are their leader, but you were once in their shoes. How did you feel? What did you wish your leader did to engage you? Were there days you felt you had ideas but no one would listen? Did you have days that you wish your VP or an Exec would acknowledge that you even worked there? Did you screw up and get someone mad or did they sit down and help you understand what you could have done better? You obviously got promoted, but has that always been the case in the jobs you've worked? Do you listen to your staff? Do you put your phone aside and focus on them? Do you show ways in which you value them for their contributions to the company? **You have the power to engage**

or disengage your team. And it starts best by remembering your own days in their shoes.

Sport is competitive. Salespeople who work in sports are competitive. They hunger and sell for that commission, that bonus. In addition to that, they hunger for the chance to make their mark. It's up to us as leaders to find ways to unleash that ability and let them make that mark rather than keep them in a robotic sales mold. How exciting for them to use their brain, build their strategy, utilize their strengths, be acknowledged in front of family and peers, and have an understanding leader!

POTATO CHIP LEADERSHIP SKILLS

CREATING GREAT SALES OPPORTUNITIES

You make a lot of calls. You set appointments. You get hung up on. You have to hit quotas. You have some contests. You know you could be making more money outside of sports, yet you wake up and do it all over again. What keeps you coming back?

An engaged sales team is one that has little turnover, a charged atmosphere, and a team whose strengths are being utilized daily. They work hard and play hard. They hit goals. They have an "All In" mentality. *They are valued.*

A team on the court practices a lot to get where they are going. They sweat, they make mistakes, they get coached, they laugh, they get frustrated, and then they do it again. Then comes the game and they are focused and ready for the challenge at hand. They celebrate wins. They talk about losses and how they can get better. They work harder. They try new techniques. And they go out to the next game and again are focused and ready for the challenge at hand. Is this not the same environment we want for our team in the office?

A sales and service team with great culture is not afraid to be a little unconventional. They know that "mixing things up" generates more enthusiasm. They know that they have a voice that is heard. They know the phone is not the only way to sell and they create new ways to sell and build relationships. And they know that they are not afraid to hold themselves accountable and share in helping their teammates be accountable. They are a team in the truest sense of the word. What makes these employees different?

- **First and foremost, they are valued.** I cannot emphasize this enough. Look at teams you have worked with. Were you truly valued or simply another person to hit goals? Did leadership ever show their appreciation or was it expected? Just like food, shelter, and clothing are physical necessities in life, being valued, appreciated, and invested in are necessities at work.

- **Invest in the staff.** The single most important job you have as leader is to invest in your staff. If you don't, nothing else will matter. No matter what your day looks like, investment in your staff needs to be a large part of it. Help them grow. Coach them. Celebrate with them. Appreciate them. Recognize their worth. Give them unique projects to help them grow more. Let go of the

"I lead, you follow" mentality and instead create a mentality along the lines of "I'm going to take you on a journey with me."

- **Listen.** The key in selling is to listen. Why do we stop as leaders? Listen to your staff. Look away from your laptop when talking with them. Stop checking your phone when you are meeting with them. Listen. What are they saying/not saying? Encourage active participation. Use some of their ideas. Let them be part of the process in this journey. Which would you prefer? Being told how and what you will sell, or being part of the process of planning what will be sold and how? Being able to share ideas and truly collaborate creates a personal investment in what you are selling. Plus, if it is part of their idea, they will not want it to fail. Once you stop listening, you create the "I lead, you follow" mentality. Robotic. No engagement.

- **Create engagement.** During no meeting, no huddle, and no conversation should all the talking be done by you as a leader. When selling, we follow the 80/20 rule: 80% of the talking done by the prospect, 20% done by us. Why change with our staff? Engagement creates spirit and energy. It creates a "we can" attitude instead of an "I have to" attitude.

- **Their strengths are recognized and utilized.** How much better is work when you can use the best part of you? Teams that recognize employees' strengths have employees who do their best work day after day. If you are utilizing your best strengths, are you not more energized and passionate? It's who we are that defines us. Who is your team? Who is each individual? Let them define themselves and grow.

- **They know there is more than one way to sell and can use all ways.** They know that they have to make calls to connect. But they also know and can use in-person methods, social media sales, large unique afterhours or morning breakfast events, walking the pavement and owning a city, and yes, even snail mail. Point is, they can mix and match and be energized at all points during the day.

- **Use power hours in an energizing and fun way.** This team may do pushups or squats prior to or even stand during a power hour to get themselves pumped and ready. Take them to the press box to make calls. Take cell phones and call from the seats in the park or court. It breaks up the day, creates new energy, and also enables them to be on their "A" game.

- **As a leader, relinquish leadership and enable the team to grow.** From letting the members lead morning huddles, to helping create contests, to having ownership of projects and meetings … leaders realize they are only as good as the team members they are leading. This goes back to engagement and the 80/20 rule. Delegating is one of the hardest things a leader does but letting go actually invites positive culture and energy.

- **They write a personal business strategy.** Writing a personal business strategy enables a team to have their personal GPS intact throughout the sales season. It gives them the guide to refer back to should they get detoured and keeps them on the right road, as well as providing a way to hold themselves accountable. They have 1:1s with you based on their business strategy—it is a living, breathing document for them and you coach them based on it.

- **They have measurable results that help them be personally accountable.** From personal business strategies to charts with their revenue goals in front of them to be colored in daily, they keep their eye on the goal. When you coach, you leave them with one or two measurable things to work on till the next coaching session. Now, instead of going into a coaching session discussing the pipeline, you are actually helping them grow and giving them something measurable they can work on and see the results.

- **They are *allowed* to grow and develop.** Want to learn how to sell premium? Want to think sponsorship? Want to help plan an event? If you are vested in the organization and giving your all, the sky is the limit for you to learn and keep growing. You are not pegged in one spot forever. How often do we keep square pegs in square holes, round pegs in round holes, and never let them experience what else it could be like? Why can't we take a great seller ready for a new experience and coach them in prospecting, identifying, meeting, creating a proposal, and learning the art of negotiating in an opportunity to sell some corporate? This is how we keep staff engaged. When they are excelling in an area, give them new opportunities. This shows you value them.

- **They have contests.** Some teams have dropped contests as "it is their job to sell." I think those who believe that have not been the ones on the phones getting hung up on or told no fifty times a day. Contests spark energy. Contests tend to bring out the spirit in sales reps. And, the more creative the better. The key is to create the contest for the team: a team goal, a team win. You don't see our players on the field/court/ice go out and play as individuals. They play as a team and celebrate wins as a team.

- **Recognize achievements.** From trips that are weekend flights to away games, to a weekend in Las Vegas, to an Academy Awards ceremony … work hard, play hard, and the hard work will continue. Even more importantly, recognize great effort or great sales. Leave them a post-it on their desk at night. Have the President leave them a voicemail on their phone recognizing an achievement. The little things help us win the big things. All because we are appreciated.

- **As a leader, how much do you know your staff?** Do you know each member's motivation? Strength? Weakness? Hot button? Side projects? Get to know your staff and you unleash the opportunities to grow them and engage them. I once had a rep whose mother had cancer. She was a single mom, so he would leave daily shortly after 5 pm to take care of her. The leadership team thought he wasn't dedicated. They never took the time to know what the problem was, how they could have supported him, or how they could take a sad situation and help make it tolerable for this poor rep. They didn't know their staff.

I have been very fortunate and honored as a consultant to work with some extremely engaged sales and service teams, teams that are allowed to be innovative, creative, and collaborative. Teams whose supervisors, managers, directors, GMs, and President are all vested in the growth and development of the members as well as achieving goals by allowing members to be part of the process. Teams who view strategy as the key to success. Teams who write their personal business strategies and take it seriously. Teams who goes after goals, week after week, not just hitting them but trying to crush them. These are teams who are truly engaged, know when they are given an opportunity and want to give back, and above all want the organization as a whole to succeed. THIS is an engaged culture.

THE SEVENTH CHIP

LET GO & SELL MORE

Welcome to today's world: Season tickets don't have the impact they used to. Long-term suites are not top of mind. Groups want more of an event than just buying tickets and showing up. Social media has an impact. Year after year, leadership teams get together and create packages they feel should be sold and give them to their sales teams to sell. Many are told not to have a personal team Twitter account. It's like going into an airless room, being given a sheet listing what you are "pitching" that night, and not being given the oxygen to do it, such as the opportunity to use your brain.

Executive teams: Think about the days when you were a sales rep. How many times did you have an idea, only you never shared it because you were told what you would sell? How frustrated did you feel? How often do you wonder, if only I could have done ___, the outcome may have been so different? Yet here we are still putting together tired packages and expecting our sales staff to have the enthusiasm to sell them. If only you could wander the sales floors and hear the reps sometimes with some excellent comments of how much more successful the sales process could be if only we could ...

News flash to leaders: A rep sells so much better when selling that which he/she had the opportunity to help create and believe in. You are not going to let an idea that you were part of fail. You will jump through hoops to make it successful. Using social media methods to sell can double their sales numbers. So why do we as executives insist on putting it together and having them sell it the way we say?

Leadership needs to realize it's okay to let go. You are only as good as the people around you. If you believe in the people you have hired, then *empower* them to be part of the process. Those in the trenches who listen to clients day in and day out can often be counted on to come up with some great ideas for alternative and more "trendy" membership packages, changes to groups, suite usage, rental packages, etc. *Collaborating* with you on this, presenting ideas, and seeing their efforts be part of the new packages will motivate the rep to feel like a more valued part of the team, and also give them the opportunity to sell something they had a say in. The effort goes up, the positive attitude goes up, and ultimately, sales go up.

A great seller will find needs and offer solutions based on parameters they are given. Instead of "pitching," they use their brain and are empowered to create packages and truly build solutions for their client ... an amazing way to sell.

What if we empowered our staff to create a revenue agreement with a client then create their own package with them around it? A package may include five sets of tickets to games, a hundred-person group outing and two rental suites, one large and one small. It doesn't fit any of the molds that we sell from, but it does offer flexibility to the client, and a great chance for a rep to find needs, fill them, and work collectively with the client. They may even find that creating a revenue bank for the client to use throughout the year works best—a $10K investment to be used as needed, when needed, during the course of the season. This can be tickets to games, a group, suite rental, or any type of mixture.

If you truly trust the people you have hired, as you should, then give them the leeway to create the best sales for you. Start simple if you feel comfortable and initially let them be part of the process, contributing ideas. As you become more comfortable, little by little, empower your reps to create sales for the future by creating for the client. For example, in a conversation with the El Paso Locomotives, the team created "The Office" package as a take on the show *The Office*. They were energized, I was energized, and a new idea was born. One of the reps really wanted to focus on small business and created a small business package of season memberships that, more importantly, gave small businesses the opportunity to market on the team's social media, getting in front of thousands of people they otherwise could not reach. He hit his season sales goal quickly. Not everyone wants 81 or 41 games, but many are willing to spend the $5K to $10K in different ways.

At the end of the day, it's all about control. We feel in control as a leader if we have this plateful of things to do that is ours. We feel in control if we tell the reps what they are selling. We feel in control if we run everything. By not empowering, not delegating, and not letting our people grow, we imply that we are the only ones capable of doing these actions. In reality, if we didn't show up for work tomorrow, the business would go on and someone else would get the tasks done.

How do we let go? I often tell leaders to keep a journal for a week of every task they do, from the time they get in until the time they leave, including anything they may do at home. List the task and they "why" of it being done. Then list the amount of time it took you to work on it. At the end of the day, list the things you needed to do or should have done to coach your team. Where did the team end up that week? Hitting the goal? Not hitting the goal?

After the end of the week, make a list. One side: things I did that are confidential or needed to be done by me only. Add up those hours. On the other side: things I did that anyone, with guidance, could have tackled. Add up those hours. Then list the amount of time spent coaching and working directly with your staff. Add up those hours. Now, looking at what could have been delegated, take those hours and add them to the amount of time spent with your team. THIS is how you should be functioning. As leaders, we have one job: to grow and develop our people. If you are a President, you should be developing your VPs. If a VP, developing your directors. If a director, developing your manager. And directors and managers: developing your team. Extra busy work that you refuse to delegate does not make you a leader. It makes you exhausted and frustrated.

Now let's look at what we can delegate. Look at your staff's strengths. Who is best for each job with proper guidance? This is your opportunity to coach them in growth and leadership: doing a project, creating check-ins for the project, turning in the results for the project when they are due. Will it be perfect? Maybe not. Will it be accurate? Make sure they double check. Will they feel valued and empowered? You bet. Will you have spent more time with them and your team? Hopefully. That's where you should be.

Now look at what you can empower them to do that they can simply report in on. Can they create some packages they want to sell? Can they create some unique ideas for social media sales? How can you let them use their gray matter? What on your list could you step back and let the team take charge of?

Letting go frees you up for the jobs you need to do: special reports, coaching 1:1 sessions, creating department strategy, getting to know your people, evaluating how each best learns, etc. Letting go actually is the first step to becoming a strong leader. We don't control our team, we support our team. Just as the coach on the court or field creates a strategy with the help of the team and then let's go and lets them play. Loosens the reigns and focus more on the coaching of each team member. This enables them to win. And isn't our goal to have our staff win?

DO GOALS EQUAL ACHIEVEMENT?

We hire intelligently. We give everyone their goals. We get excited. They start selling. And then they plateau. Goals aren't being hit and, instead of looking at ourselves, we are frustrated with them.

A smart leader will assess and come up with an action plan. An autocratic leader will blame the staff and expect them to stay longer hours, make more calls, etc. The question as a leader should be: Why are they not hitting goals?

Three questions come to mind right at the start:

*   Who has set the goals? Was the team part of the process or told?

*   Were the goals attainable or were they unrealistic?

*   Do they understand what hitting these goals does for them personally and for the organization? Have they been part of understanding where the organization is going and do they see their piece of the puzzle in this?

Asking those questions, we find why people don't hit goals, and it generally stems from our leadership.

Fear of failure and/or success. Leadership tends to play the blame game or the play favorites and either way is a loss for the team members. With failure, they will get blamed and called out. With success, they will be favored and it will further destroy culture.

Lack of understanding about goal setting. It's not about giving them a piece of paper with a number and date on it, filled out by month by the leader as to what they bring in. It's about creating your own process for the long term. It's about learning what the visionary or strategic plan is for the next 3 years. It's understanding where we've been and where we're going. It's about buy-in. It's about stating the goal for the year and then each rep being given an individual goal. It's about the rep breaking down their goal by month as to how they feel they will bring in the revenue under your guidance. It's about learning to be accountable and create strategy and process. And it starts with you the leader to teach this.

Lack of commitment to the goal. This generally stems from not having clear understanding, clarity, and accountability. It means there is most likely not an action plan that was asked for by the leader. You can't be accountable if you're not committed.

Analysis paralysis. So many teams are now focused on the analytics that they are removing the personality from the process. A great leader will balance both.

They've failed to plan. As a leader, your role is to guide them through creating their strategy, process and execution.

Reactionary goals. Here's what you have to bring in this month but oh wait, we need to sell more tickets for the next game. Stop everything and try and get some tickets sold for Saturday. This is poor planning, follow up, and communication on the leader's part. In this instance, you set them up to fail long term.

Before we get upset with a team for not hitting goals, go through the process you set up. Have you followed through all the areas or did you simply throw the number at them and tell them what to do? Have you been coaching them through their processes? Have you focused on call quantity versus call quality? Have you helped them understand the pipeline process?

Before we ever get upset with the team for not functioning, we have to first look in the mirror and ask ourselves: Have we done everything we could and should have to develop them, prepare them, and coach them?

POTATO CHIP LEADERSHIP SKILLS

WHAT TODAY'S REPS WANT

What has been most energizing for me as I work with sales teams from sports and entertainment is the fact that they are not afraid to say they want to be part of the process. They want to be building a strategy and using their creativity. They want to (gasp!) use their brain. What happened?

For so many years, we have been reliving the 1980s and 90s, when there were fewer entertainment options, teams were building mega-facilities, and sports entertainment was *the* place to be. We didn't really sell as much as take orders. We called from lists we were given. We were told to make one hundred calls a day. We were given a script. And we were to close, close, close.

Today's market is different. There are so very many options as to how to spend your weeknights and weekends. Tastes have changed. High-pressure sales have gone the way of the used car salesmen. But while times changed, our strategy for selling hasn't. We still ask for the one hundred calls a day and many still use scripts, a la "here's a list and close, close, close." Why? Because people are afraid to step out of their comfort zone.

Let's think about this.

Here we are knowing things have to change, telling our sales staff to step out of their comfort zone, yet making sure they do the same things they've always done. Is it any wonder why we, as leaders, are afraid to try something different? One of the key things in leadership is to remember that we are only as good as the team around us. Put a strong, creative, collaborative, and energizing team around you and they will not fail you. You will look like a hero.

So, what should the future sales staff look like?

- **Empowered and allowed to be part of the process.** Who makes decisions? Normally, the people in charge who aren't in the trenches listening to clients. If any of you have kids, you get this. If you tell them to do this and that, do you always get the results you hoped? Generally, after a while, it goes in one ear and out the other. Now *ask* your kids for their input. Suddenly, they set the time frame to get things done, they start managing their day better and life becomes smoother. No different with your sales team. Teams who tell their sales staff: Here is the pricing **we've** decided upon, here is the strategy **we've** picked, and here are the packages **we've** chosen. We are doing the *telling*. And results are average at best. The teams who have their members help create the strategy for pricing ideas, how they would like to sell it, and the packages they feel would work find engagement, energy, and sales results. When it is *their* idea, do you think they are going to let it fail? Of course not. Suddenly, you have goals hit and a more energized team in your salesroom.

As leaders, do more listening and less talking. Use ideas they have. Make them part of the process.

- **Sales by prospecting.** Interns can call from lists … why do we need sales staff? Calling from lists often finds us getting robotic, not using passion in our discussions, and dialing for dollars. Prospecting enables you to use your brain, research, find who OUR people are, and believe they are a fit. Prospecting and calling for an appointment start the process of relationship building, whereas calling from lists becomes impersonal.

A

s leaders, teach your team how to understand who our people are, where they might be, how to find them, and then how to find people like them. This makes your team so much more valuable.

- **Supersizing in creative ways.** The best opportunity to use the brain comes in supersizing. How can we supersize season sales? Who can we go after to supersize group sales? This gets the creative juices flowing and the brain sparking. And this creates energy. Energy that is needed in the department. Enthusiasm. Passion. As leaders, help your team get beyond selling the one by one by one and learn how to sell in bulk.

Let them understand the process from start to finish and really run their own small business.

- **Utilizing social media.** Why are so many teams afraid of this? Most likely they don't understand it. They view it more as a Millennial and Generation Z shortcoming instead of a Millennial and Generation Z tool. I've had teams whose reps have utilized group leaders on a Twitter account and cross sold season. Reps who have utilized season holders on Twitter and cross sold groups. I have some who are starting groups on Facebook for their season and for their group leaders to maximize sales opportunities. I have some who have utilized Instagram to draw awareness and ultimately sales. Let them be creative and create new ways to sell. More often than not, the reason teams give me for not wanting to use it is because they can't measure it as well as call volume. Wrong reason!!!

As leaders, trust is important. Trust your team to utilize social media instead of fearing it. With trust comes accountability.

- **Getting out of the office** and meeting with people enables one to build relationships. How many phone calls does it take to build a relationship? If ever? Have a meeting with a prospect and you are already months ahead of numerous phone calls.

As a leader, you may fear out-of-office meetings as they miss "call volume." In reality, an out-of-office meeting should count as twenty calls. Why? When you schedule a meeting, the client expects an ask to be made. You're already ahead of the game.

- **Texting clients.** Think about it. Back in the day, we would quickly blast out an email if we had something exciting for our client. Nowadays, most of us text our urgency, so why not the sales rep? If the customer or prospect is comfortable with it, let our staff be comfortable with it. The key: Ask our clients for their preferred communication, then follow it.

As a leader, embrace the opportunity to connect with our clients in the way they choose, even if it goes against what you are comfortable with.

- **Run their own small business.** Reps today want ownership of their small business. They want to be empowered to create ideas and make them work. They offer unusual ways to sell to large groups of people. They want to carve paths of their own. Is there anything really wrong with this?

As leaders, make sure their ideas are well thought out and let them test them. This is how we move the business forward.

- **Balance.** After watching their parents (us!) both work, miss events of theirs at school because of work, and bring work home to invade the one space that should be separate from it, is it any wonder reps today want work/life balance? Yet as leaders, we fight it because that's all we know. Whether you have 40 or 81 games, does every rep have to work every game? Can they not rotate and also leave at staggered times? Can it not be more important that they have relaxed downtime, so they come to work the next day a bit more refreshed instead of dragging? We still have to sell when the team is on the road but do we expect them to stay long hours then too?

As leaders, we need to make sure our team is refreshed, happy, and ready to start their day.

- **Fair wage.** With student loans, car payments, and so many bills, is it no wonder they leave us? We are a business just like other industries. They are leaving us for them. We need to step up and manage our finances just like they do.

As leaders, make sure your reps are paid fairly with strong incentives. Give them the same opportunities they would have in the business world. Break the mold, as some teams are already doing.

I love today's sales reps and find them some of the most energizing I have ever worked with. They challenge me with ideas, and that's a great thing. I challenge them. And they respond by coming up with even better ideas. It's time to take our reps to the next level of selling. All we need to do is provide the light bulb … they will be more than happy to turn it on!

Potato Chip Trainers

Changing Culture: Observe your team for a week.

1. Do they come in energized ready to go daily or come in, sit down, and start checking emails?

2. Is there a "let me help" attitude or does no one volunteer?

3. Create a checklist of areas you see/hear throughout the week that need increased positive energy and passion.

4. Then list ideas of what you can do to help create it.

Letting Go: Create a one-week journal of all of your activities. Also list time spent with reps. Keep track of minutes/hours dedicated to each activity.

1. At the end of the week, make three lists: part of my job, busy work, time spent with each rep for the week.

2. What can you let go? Add up that time. Put that time into the time spent with each rep column. Do you see how investment in your people occurs? We *make* time to make it happen. Looking at the busy work list, as projects come up, know the strengths of your people.

3. Which can you delegate to which reps as a learning experience? Evaluate every project you get. What is important for you to do, what can be a learning tool? Take the time from that and mark it on your calendar to be spent with your team.

Know your staff. Make a list of each member. Identify their passion and side projects. Figure out their hot buttons.

1. In your next 1:1 find out more about them (how do they spend weekends, what is their favorite hobby, etc).

2. How much time do you spend with each?

3. How have you recognized them? How can you serve them?

4. Have you spent active listening time? Do you give them respect?

Be the leader your team needs. What does your staff want in a job, in a leader?

1. Create a log of qualities.

2. Where do you need improving?

Create a positive environment. Identify a positive for everyone on your team. Identify negative(s).

1. What makes it a negative?

2. What is the type of employee you want? What type of room do you want?

3. Who best exemplifies this? Why? What are the qualities?

4. Who does not exemplify this? Why not? How can you bring them aboard your bus?

The Eighth
Potato Chip

JOB OR PASSION

In working with teams and companies across the country, I tend to do a lot of one-on-one work with the staff: finding their strengths, unleashing their creativity, and encouraging strategic thinking. It's like finding/hiring a whole new staff at times when I'm done. As a whole, the industry tends to focus too much on "this is how we do it" and everyone coming in to the company gets put into the same mindset. How much better things could be, how much more energy we could generate, how many more seats could be utilized, how much more revenue could be gained, and how much more engaged would your staff be if instead of saying, "This is how we do it," we said, "This is how we do it now: Put together a plan and let's talk about how YOU would do it."

How powerful and creative our associates can become when allowed to engage their brain and use their strengths versus performing the status quo method. How much better could we keep staff? Is there really only one way to sell? One way to market? One way to embrace technology? What better way to have them truly engaged in the company/team than by feeling they have a true contribution to make!

How to get started?

Have your members create their quarterly business strategy each year and take ownership of their work

- Why should the executive team be the only ones to create a business strategy for everyone else to follow? What if we engaged the staff to create theirs?

- You will need to shed the "closed door secrets" mentality and share the 3-year strategy. They need to know where the team/company has been, what renovation strategies are in place, where it wants to go, and what they want to accomplish the coming year. What failed? What worked? What was the

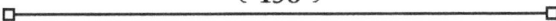

customer engagement like? They need to truly know the team/company they are working for. Then they need to ask themselves: What personal things did I do that failed or worked? What can I do the upcoming year, quarter by quarter, that can create the vision of the company and hold myself accountable? They need to learn as much as they can about the company and take a personal interest in it.

- Create their quarterly personal business strategy and present it to both the Director and the VP. This enables them to take personal pride and accountability in their role. An associate will succeed when they are part of the process and the decision making. When they create a business plan that may not fit the ideal mold but has merit and should be tried, they will not let it fail. It is theirs. They have buy-in.

- As they create this plan, their strengths will come in to play. Employees can't get much more engaged or happy than when they are using their best skillset to accomplish a goal that they have helped create.

Meet with the associates weekly for 1:1 coaching sessions

- Express personal interest and don't wait for the dreaded evaluations.

- Meeting weekly, you have the opportunity to give affirmation, assistance if needed, help them with their plan, and high five accomplishments. Evaluations won't be dreaded, as there will be coaching done on a continual basis. If there is help and coaching needed, you can stay engaged and keep the enthusiasm going by assisting. This sets them up for success for themselves, for you, and for the company.

- Coaching sessions should provide measurable ways to grow. Each session should not focus on pipeline, but rather on something in their technique you have observed in which you can help them grow. It should be their measurable focus for the week. For example, closing techniques.

- You will be surprised at how much more engaged YOU will become!

Encourage ideas in weekly/monthly meetings

- In sales, we make an opening statement, then be quiet. Why not do the same as leaders in a meeting? We tend to ramble forever.

- State what you'd like to improve/change and then turn it over to your staff to create the ideas of how. Let them pick one or two to focus on for the upcoming month/quarter. Again, if it's THEIR idea, they won't let it fail. Give them the opportunity to talk about the idea, the how, discuss why it may/may not work, what pitfalls might they expect and, if it's a possibility, let them create the plan of "how." Isn't this the essence of sales? Presenting a thought then letting THEM talk?

- Create a CEO (Chief Energy Officer) at the end of the meeting to follow through with the staff the upcoming month/quarter and take charge of the execution. Let the CEO report to you weekly on what is going well or not. This enables people to be leaders and start to learn how to manage in a non-threatening way.

- Sometimes we get so involved in creating so many processes, so many hoops to jump through to get a thought from idea to fruition, that what used to be excitement at the creative process and using our brains becomes, "Why bother?" Just fit the mold. Do as they say. This is how it's done. And we wonder why there is staff turnover? Why we lose not just one or two of the best, but suddenly more and more?

We hire people. The whole person. People who have a brain with ideas, strengths, a desire to make a difference. Let's go back to hiring the whole person. Let's enable them to bring all they have to the table. Let's allow them to get engaged. Whether a team or company, from the custodial staff to the CEO, let's help them feel passion and not just a job. Let's create a buzz in the workplace again—the ideas flowing, strengths and teamwork coming to the surface. Suddenly, you don't need to hire. People want to come to you.

And in the end, success. A successful company that can truly say … WE did it.

THE EIGHTH CHIP

KILLING THE COMFORT ZONE

Just before graduating from nursing school, my Director of Nursing pulled me aside and told me what I was quickly realizing: "Kathy, there is no room for creativity in nursing." What was I thinking!?! I would have to stifle what was one of my best strengths to fulfill a career. No surprise that after 5 years I moved on.

Fast forward to the 2000s. I was introducing Stop Selling Tickets to some VPs of teams. I asked them why they continued measuring success by focusing on one hundred calls a day. Their answer: They can't measure the results of a creative process, and because that's the way it's always been done.

This is definitely Einstein's definition of insanity when it comes to sports and entertainment. A hundred calls a day no matter what. And that gets us ...? Are our stadiums and arenas sold out with that thought process? Of course, we have to make calls ... but there are four results we should have from that call: a time and day for a next call, a meeting with a time and day, a sale, or a no.

What if instead we focused on measuring revenue by week, not by the calls or the close, but just the revenue, and encouraged our staff to use their strengths to bring it in? What if we encouraged our staff to build and write a strategy that works with their strengths and focus on their execution of that strategy? What if, when we meet with them for 1:1s, we talk about what is working and what is not? Which parts of their strategy are showing success and how can we tweak areas that aren't? Many of us don't because it's out of OUR comfort zone as leaders.

In 1980s and 90s, when sports and entertainment ruled the world, it was easy to make those calls per day and close, close, close. But now people and companies have choices. They want to weigh their options. They want to know if what you have to offer will fit their needs. They want to do business with someone they can trust.

What will it take to break the cycle? It will take leadership that has a backbone and a strategy. Leadership that is not afraid to take that risk. I meet with so many teams whose staff is so ready to do it differently: meetings, social selling, snail mail, calls, group events, morning coffee meetings, or afterhours group meetings. I work with them. I teach them how. And then they aren't allowed to do it. Why? Because it's out of their supervisor's comfort zone.

We know Inside Sales is meant to make a lot of calls. They have to establish rhythm and practice. Then they get promoted and are expected to produce large numbers, and our only measure is call volume. We haven't encouraged them to meet with clients on their turf. We haven't encouraged them to assess needs. More often than not, we've only taught them how to close.

Let's do a little self-check as leaders and see how we might break the cycle:

Start with the business strategy. What creative ways can they come up with to sell other than dialing for dollars? How can they set meetings? How can they speak to groups of people? How would they utilize social selling? How could they incorporate all of this into a day? Let them use their mind and share how they feel they can be successful.

B2B meetings. Lately, I have heard from leaders who do not want their staff setting up a meeting for B2B as "it will take too long, just close." I want to sell those seats for the long term, not resell them year after year. Let your staff member have those meetings. Let them find the needs and offer the product that makes the most sense. Build on that year after year.

Speaking of finding needs, **let's stop selling and start listening**. Let's let our clients tell us what would make their lives better, or the lives of their sales staff better. Let's figure out how we can bridge the gap of those needs and make a strong sale that is customized for them instead of selling the same one year after year.

Social selling and snail mail. Not comfortable with social selling because maybe they're "goofing around on social media instead of working?" In this day and age, "goofing around on social media" actually can be selling. Break down the barrier. As a leader, don't be afraid to learn. Have them teach you the why, the how, and the expected results. I encouraged one of my salespeople to go ahead and create their own Twitter account to work with people attending as a group. After about 6 months of engagement on Twitter, this person converted so many of those people to season and other groups. Their approach brought a greater success than "a call at a time."

Coaching our staff. So many 1:1 meetings go over the same thing: you're not making enough calls, you have to ask for the sale, you're not sharing all our benefits. We could have robo calls do that stuff. Let's start coaching our staff. They wrote their business strategy—let's coach them through it. Let's help them understand how to reevaluate when a strategy isn't working. Let's coach them on the business meetings they want. Let's coach them on how to listen and give them one potato chip at a time instead of throwing the bag at the client. Let's coach them on snail mail and social media, or if needed, have them coach us.

Invest in multiple trainings and encourage them to attend trainings. Here we go. We did our yearly training. That's it until next year. Meanwhile, a week later, we are back to our usual ways. Training should be twofold: first for the staff, and then for leadership so that they can encourage the staff to follow through on what they were just taught. What I encourage is using all the talent you have in ways that work best for you and then create the process and write the strategy. If we are using analytics now, why can't we encourage our sales staff to use their minds to create a strategic process? And why not use a couple different trainings a year? The reinforcement and the new ideas are all like a breath of fresh air when the staff is mid-year and needing to be re-energized. And if our staff wants to attend a workshop somewhere, why do we discourage it? They are trying to get better for you and the organization!

As leaders, you all had to start somewhere. You all had a boss who you wanted to try new ideas with. And you either were permitted to or your idea got squashed. If you did try something new, then give that same opportunity to your staff. If you got squashed, then break that cycle and give your staff the freedom to use the strengths they have. We have to stop being afraid of stepping out of that big bad comfort zone and huff and puff and blow the barriers down.

There may not be room for creativity in nursing, but there sure is room for creativity in selling and understanding in leadership. Time to let Einstein know you are breaking the cycle. Make the change! Invest in your people. Really get to understand what each member of your sales staff can bring to the table.

POTATO CHIP LEADERSHIP SKILLS

LET'S CHANGE THE MESSAGE

I once worked with a member of an analytics team who told the sales team that he would rather have one person in the facility spending a million dollars than have a million customers coming out spending $1 each. He also added his dislike of smaller partial plan holders "who waste our time and don't deserve nearly the same treatment, as they're fickle anyway." This was a person who would often say, "We don't need them. Just go get a big sale." During renewals it was an attitude of "Fine, let them go. We don't need them." Needless to say, this was a very depressed sales team and damage control was frequently being done.

These were very challenging and depressing statements made to the sales team. To say it hurt culture would be an understatement. It created a team that went through the motions, continually looking over their shoulder. Not a great environment for sales.

My question is: what message are you sending YOUR sales team?

I have teams who have hugely successful sales reps in terms of revenue and hitting goals who are being reprimanded because they are bringing in money but not making seventy calls a day to do it. What?? There are probably a lot of teams out there reading this saying, "I want those reps on my team!" Yet the message you are actually sending is "I'm glad you are crushing your goals but my metrics for success is seventy calls a day, so you are not successful." Conflicting message? Frustrated rep? Reps who will probably leave sports shaking their head?

Let's change the message to focusing on a guideline of metrics: here is the goal, here are ways to achieve it, and let's *watch your growth week by week and see where you need help. Some people are not good at seventy calls a day, but turn them loose on social media or in person and they could hit their goal in a month.*

I've had leaders complain to successful reps that, again, it's great that their goals are being crushed, but their hustle scores aren't where they need to be, so they will probably not be promoted. Again, a measure straight out of the 80s that we still use and not very well.

Let's change the message to *setting a team goal for the week, and everyone's name on the board with a personal goal for the week. Let's focus on hitting the goal with various measures in place as above. We can include in-person meetings/calls/social media/etc. But the ultimate measure is hitting the goal.*

There are leaders who bring trainers aboard and then never step in to see or hear what is being trained. What is the message sent? "You can listen, but when it's done, it's still being done my way." Or "I did my job and got a trainer. Now just sell according to my metrics."

Let's change the message to *let's all hear some new ways to sell and discuss afterwards how we can best implement them.*

What about the leader who tells their team: "Here is what we are selling. Go sell it." What is the message there? Kind of like the hamster who is to run that little treadmill trying to get that treat. No input, no teamwork, no empowerment. Just do it.

Let's change the message to *here's what needs to be sold. Let's talk about the best ways you feel we can attack this and put a plan together to do it this week.*

I've experienced the negative leader. Sell by intimidation. That's a really great message to send out to your team.

Let's change the message *to here's the goal. As a team, you have a half hour to decide how you are going to attack it, and how much each of you will be accountable for. You can also decide a reward for the week for hitting it.*

Sometimes it's a trickledown effect ... our boss yells at us, and in reaction we respond to the sales team in the same way.

Let's change the message to one of respond instead of react.

My point is, what we say and how we act as leaders will have a direct result on our staff. It will result in turnover, in goals not being hit, in frustration levels, lack of passion, and poor culture. We all need to look at the message we are sending.

Is it upbeat? Is it inclusive? Are we empowering? Are we coaching? Are we encouraging our reps to use their brain and be creative in methods of sales? Are we open minded to change? Are we understanding or are we forgetful of the fact that our reps hear a lot of "no" before they get a "yes"? Do we remember that in sports, people certainly aren't there because of the pay, but rather the passion?

Most importantly, do we remember that each and every client who our reps bring aboard is so very important to them? They worked hard to build that relationship, be it a premium or a partial plan. They want to respect that relationship and continue to nurture it as we don't know what the future investment will be.

A good message here *is to encourage your reps to have coffee with those they have sold to occasionally. Keep the relationship going. Encourage them to ask their buyers for help to find more like them.*

Communication has a direct impact on performance. What messages have you been sending YOUR sales reps?

WHAT COMES OUT OF OUR PEARLY WHITES?

I asked a leader to put together a personal strategy for the team as to how to achieve their particular goal. He did, but it turned out to be a personal strategy for himself. He heard the first part but not the second. Before he left, I should have made sure he understood what I was asking of him.

How many times have we asked someone to do something only to have them do something entirely different? How many times have we failed to delegate because they "won't get it right." Is it them … or us as leaders?

One of the most important things a leader will do is communicate. Clear communication sets the table for ideas, planning, and success. The key word is "clear." Oftentimes, we imply things and assume our message is loud and clear, only to find our reps going off in a totally different direction.

I get this because I've been guilty of it myself! So many times, I would tell someone something, anticipating it would be carried out, only to find that they heard something different. Little by little, it made me realize that when leading, my words were important but how I said it and explained it become so much more important.

Let's look at messaging. I see it in two ways: one in our coaching sessions, and one that is general.

In our coaching sessions, we may give our reps a few measurable things to work on. There are different ways we say it. In one way, we use over-inflated words that are foreign to our reps. I once had a leader who was so impressed with his own choice of words that my staff and I had absolutely no idea what he was saying. I finally had to ask him to speak in ways that we could understand. Yes, it's great to elevate your audience, but it's also important to communicate with your audience so they understand.

In our coaching sessions, we give a few measurable tasks. As others are writing them down, they are jotting down what they think they hear. It is crucial to have them repeat it back to you. The easiest way to do that is to put in on yourself and say, "Sometimes, what I'm thinking doesn't necessarily equate to how I'm saying it. What did you hear, so that I'm sure we are on the same page?" Clarifying things early on allows you to contribute to your team's success instead of their frustration.

To boil it down even more, before they leave ask, "So what two things will you be working on?"

Then there is what we communicate to our team. We tend to speak in numbers or vague generalities. For example, we tell our team we need to sell more season memberships, so make sure your pipeline is full. The reps go back and do just that. They want to make you happy and do what you ask. They fill in a kazillion leads, but those are prospects not a pipeline. Pipelines are the qualified prospects we put into it. So, what are you asking? For more prospects or more qualified prospects to put into the pipeline? Do they realize the difference? Are you sure what you are asking is being received the same way?

Another example can be when we put an emphasis on our hustle board. Our message to our reps is this is what you need to hit for success every week. Yet we are frustrated they are not closing. Is that what our emphasis is? How could this be worded differently? Are we clearly defining our messaging that the hustle board brings the skillset, and these are some of the tools to get to our ultimate goal, which is to close? And how are we closing? Isn't that an even more important question or message?

For those of us with kids, we may say, "Go clean your room." They pick up a few things, shove some under the bed, and go on their way. This is not what you intended. But did you clearly communicate?

Is your communication with your team interactive? Do you encourage their ideas instead of solely giving your ideas and the "Here is what we are going to do," approach? Do you feel it's like a day with Charlie Brown and the teacher—"Wah wah wah …"

Time to redesign how you converse and engage!

Do you use the word "YOU" too much? *You* need to make more calls. *You* need to focus on ___. *You* are coming to work late too much. If as a leader you are coaching someone, put the *you* into the sentence instead of starting the sentence. For example: "The best way to get your number up is to increase the number of qualified prospects and *you can do* this by increasing your calls." Or, "Here is what I suggest *you focus on* during power hours to help you increase your pipeline." Or, "I can't help but notice that *you are arriving to work* during or after our huddle the past three out of five mornings." There is a huge difference between the two styles of communication. One comes across critical; the other comes across as a trusted leader/advisor.

Sarcasm as communication rarely works. There are times it can be very funny; other times it can be demeaning. Sarcasm is often felt as a personal attack, which often the leader did not intend. I have had many reps who were excellent but left their team because the sarcastic comments the leader thought were funny were grating on staff and truly demoralizing. Save the sarcasm for a moment when true humor is intended.

Lack of communication is the worst possible case. In my study of how many sports sales reps and leaders were leaving, poor leadership/lack of and poor communication were the number one reason. Think about it. If the coach on the basketball court sent the team out to play the game with no plan in place that was clearly communicated, would they be a cohesive unit looking for the win or everybody running around hoping to get the win? They may figure it out on their own and they may not. This is why the coach calls a timeout and has a whiteboard and game plan. It's clear communication. Here is the process to follow. Do we give that clear communication and game plan or assume they are all on our page?

Telling our staff, "This is the goal, you have to hit this goal, and together we will do it," is nice. More importantly, considering them part of the business and explaining why we want to hit this goal and what it means to the visionary plan of this organization is a much clearer and inclusive conversation.

Let's take the guesswork out of our communication and make sure what we are saying is what our staff is hearing instead of sending them on a wild goose chase. Let's help them feel part of the process and make sure they clearly understand the process being asked of them. Let's move the organization forward.

POTATO CHIP LEADERSHIP SKILLS

GOALS FOR THE SAKE OF GOALS

Somewhere, in the early 2000s, someone decided that setting a revenue goal isn't the answer ... setting a *stretch* revenue goal is the answer. Huh?

Let's look at how our revenue goals are set to start with. Generally, a yearly budget is discussed. Simplified, each revenue-generating department looks at what their piece of the puzzle is and creates their revenue goal. Along the way, in the past 10 years or so, the *stretch* goal was created. The team is given a goal and a stretch goal. And what happens with this?

Sales reps hit their initial goal. No kudos. No "you did it." Instead, the focus is on the stretch goal. If you don't hit that, then you didn't hit goal. But wait ... I hit goal, just not the stretch goal. Doesn't matter. You didn't hit goal.

When I work with sales teams, I encourage sales reps to create their own goal for the upcoming season prior to their director giving them revenue goals. Often, the goal they set is higher than that set by their manager. If they have done a strong strategic plan, know what and when they sold the year prior, know when the bulk of money comes in, they can pretty much go month by month and know what more can be added on for the upcoming year. But then we come in and say great, what's going to be your stretch goal? Reps will look at me and roll their eyes when I ask what goal is ... the one that is there or the one they really want us to hit? What a confusing message.

What is a stretch goal? It's defined as an additional goal set for a campaign **in case you hit your initial funding goal.** Please note: "hit your initial funding goal." Help me understand here, why are we not thanking our reps for hitting goal? They hit the original funding goal. Is it our desire to simply not let them rest on their laurels and make sure they sell more?

I have no problem with a stretch goal if the original goal is recognized and appreciated. But to simply give the two goals and tell reps they have not hit goal because they didn't hit the stretch goal is demotivating and, quite frankly, not honest. How many of our teams on the field/court/ice/pitch win, then are told, "Wait ... we have a stretch number for you to be able to win so we're going to continue the game until you score 12 more points." If we are satisfied winning on the field, then why do we change the rules for the game in the office? What to do?

My suggestions are two: one, do away with multiple goals. Make the stretch goal their, period, if this is what you want them to do to start with. Don't use negative motivation to get to the number you wanted originally. Second, empower your staff. Here is your goal. Period. Hit it prior to the end of the season. Once hit, it's time for you, as leader, to coach one on one. Here is how much time we have left. Yes, we want you to prospect for the upcoming season, but we also would like you to set a new goal for the remaining time. Empower the rep. Let them create a stretch goal with you. Give them some ownership of their small business.

In my mailbag, I get notes from reps who have been fired for hitting their goal but not the stretch goal. This is a mixed message, and one that eats away at culture, which is another question I get. So, let's create an environment where goals are set, encouraged, celebrated, and, if needed, stretched together. Even if you set the stretch goal as the goal, and stretch it even further once hit. Let's take away the two-goal system, create a unified goal, and celebrate winning.

Potato Chip Trainers

For the next sales meeting:

1. Give the team a topic that you want to discuss. Ask them to bring ideas of how to make the topic work.

2. Jot all ideas down on a whiteboard.

3. Go through pros and cons of each idea with them and expectations

4. Have team vote on what they feel is the best way to go after it the upcoming month, then have them develop their strategy as to "how."

5. This is now their plan.

For coaching sessions during this time:

1. Create one or two measurable items specific to that rep that they can work on to help them achieve the goal they set forth.

Moving into new territory:

1. List three things that you are a creature of habit about because you've "always made sure it was done that way."

2. Put a plan together as to how you can ask the team to suggest changes for the way they do these things. Let them decide a way to change they would like.

3. Let them put the plan into action, letting go of the past and having them teach you the results of the present. Look to how you can enhance these ideas.

Communication:

1. Before a meeting either with the team or a coaching 1:1 ends, ask the staff to:

2. Repeat the consensus of the discussion

3. Repeat the steps that are to be taken

4.   Listen to hear if you are communicating clearly

Passion:

1.   Look at your team. Who comes in energized daily or comes in, sits down, and starts checking emails?

2.   Create a checklist of areas in which you can create more positive energy.

3.   List ideas of what you can do to create that change.

Goal Setting:

1.   Ask each team member what their goal is. If they don't know it off the top of their head, it has not been communicated clearly.

2.   Set one goal. This is the number they are working toward. Monthly, have them list ways to hit the monthly goal on a whiteboard. This will help keep them grounded to the goal.

The Ninth
Potato Chip

OWNING MISTAKES

How many times as a leader have you felt you had to have all the answers? You feel you have to be perfect. So, there is no chance of error.

When there is a mentality of "no room for error," what happens is that the leader becomes ineffective. Decisions that staff need made sometimes take days, weeks, months—if they're ever made. The leader is trying to find a perfect decision. In this mentality, the blame game also starts. Not wanting to take responsibility, the leader puts the onus on the staff, their leader, anyone but themselves. Trust is quickly broken and there is a lack of respect by the team. They may like the leader as a person but find them ineffective and worthless as a leader. Culture becomes broken, staff becomes frustrated, and totals go down. There's no visible energy in the room and work becomes … work.

In order for a leader to become effective, one of the areas we have to perfect is owning mistakes.

Accountability: If we want to show we are a responsible leader, then we have to be accountable.

Honesty: Our staff wants to trust us so we have to have integrity in order to be trusted. With that, we own up to the mistake. This is honesty in action. Don't shift the blame if it is really on you. Don't make excuses. Don't shift the blame, even if there is more than one person responsible. Own up to your portion as a leader. Admitting error doesn't make us weak, it actually makes us human and helps our staff realize we are human too. How we handle our mistakes speaks volumes as to how we lead our team.

No hiding: Don't hide it until it festers. Be upfront with it and others will respect you. More importantly, the quicker acknowledged, the quicker it can be remedied.

Apologize: Did we hurt someone in the process? Did we set the team back by our mistake? Apologizing may not take away the pain, but it will give you respect.

Solutions: As a leader, we tell our staff to come to us with their problems and have a potential solution or two ready. It's not different when we make the mistake. We need to make sure we have a solution or two that can help correct this. Delegating it to someone else to fix is not only poor leadership, but a break in trust that is hard to earn back.

Move on: How many times do we let this mistake eat away at us weeks later? Control what you can control. It happened, you acknowledged it, it's done, and you've created a solution. Now move on. As a leader if you let it fester, it will spill over onto your team. Your team is fearful of ever making a mistake because they can see how you handle it and you will hold it against them for weeks on end.

I've had leaders who would never acknowledge a mistake but rather send their team through mazes to try and fix it and cover it up.

These are the leaders the team had no respect for. They felt they were always doing busy work that wasn't for the good of the organization, but for the sake of cleaning up a mess.

How many times have we, as leaders, goofed and asked our staff to call the person and fix it?

On the flip side, note how many times our staff asks us to call someone, as they can't seem to get the message through to them … this tells me that they may not have been completely honest with them and don't want to have to deliver the news. Who did they learn this from? Have they seen you, as a leader, take ownership or have they seen you delegate?

How you treat your mistakes sends a huge message to the staff should they make a mistake. We all make mistakes. Actually, we should. Not life threatening, of course, but mistakes mean we took a chance. There is nothing wrong with that. And THAT is the message we want to convey. It's okay to take a chance. If the chance fails, then what are the steps to acknowledging it, fixing it, and moving on?

This is a message that will help you and your team throughout their career and throughout life. This may be the biggest impact you may have with your team. Make sure you handle it wisely.

CONFIDENCE › ARROGANCE

What makes some leaders come across as arrogant while others come across as confident? What is the difference?

As Scott Berkun tells us, "An arrogant person only feels smart if someone else feels stupid. A confident person feels competent from the inside out." What we usually find is a confident person will be calmer, less reactionary, and more insightful. The arrogant person will be reactionary and look down at others versus working with others.

How do we find confidence without arrogance?

Oftentimes, people will not have the necessary confidence early on to lead so they do what they think will make them come across as "smart." They talk over people, they put their ideas out there without letting others have a thought, their body language is one of putting themselves front and center. When given a choice between an overconfident person and a less confident person, teams often follow the less confident as they feel they can trust them more. In essence, being comfortable in your own skin is key. You don't have to say, "This is me ... now I'm going to try to control you." But rather, "This is me, and we'll work together to bring our best strengths out."

We all are confident. We just don't always realize it. Think about the times you are happiest. The times you feel you are at your best. This is when you are confident. Why? What makes you happy right then? That is the mental place you need to be at to lead others.

Confidence doesn't mean we have to be the best. Confidence means we don't know it all so we hire the best we can to be around us and together we will achieve the impossible. Often I will tell a rep, "I'm so jealous in a good way! That idea is stellar!!!" I don't have all the answers. None of us do. That's why we lead and work with teams. We encourage them to help us create the best possible scenario.

Leaders who are arrogant tend to actually have low self-esteem. Their arrogance is their cover for what they feel are their inadequacies. As a leader, we need to meet our inadequacies head on. Figure them out. Find steps to improve them. This is part of our growth process. Confident leaders are aware of their shortcomings and are working to fix them. They know when to pull back and regroup before making a statement.

Arrogant leaders lecture and preach instead of listening and conversing. If we find ourselves doing all the talking, we come across as someone who is full of themselves and drones on and on and on. Rarely does anyone on our team listen when we come across that way. After the first few words, it becomes background noise. A confident leader will have a two-way conversation and engage their team.

Always wanting to have the last word or the better idea comes with arrogant leaders. They rarely acknowledge the ideas of others even if they're great ideas. What happens then is that the team becomes quiet, lacks participation, and becomes robotic. Culture is quiet and uneasy. The confident leader doesn't force the ideas. They bring their team along on the journey.

Sometimes we have success quickly and our confidence is quickly flipped to arrogance. I have met a number of leaders who rose through the ranks rapidly, and with each rise they became more self-absorbed and less tolerant of those who reported to them. They felt they had all the answers because of their quick rise. A confident leader will appreciate their success but realize their rise is most often due to those around them. Nothing creates a leader like a solid team that has success!

Arrogant leaders rarely look at their team or the individual they are talking to. They generally are looking all over, acting as if they have more important things to do. A confident leader looks directly at their team or the individual, sending the message that they are the most important person to them right now and they are focused on the conversation at hand.

While we strive for positivity in leadership, the mindset of arrogance or arrogance can either bring the positive or the negative. A confident leader breeds an atmosphere of positivity, happiness, teamwork. An arrogant leader brings an atmosphere of negativity, distrust, and isolation.

How do we change this?

Self-evaluation is essential. Evaluate yourself after meetings. Ask a mentor to evaluate you. Compare the two.

- Every time you recognize an arrogant moment, practice humility. Don't respond until you have recognized the arrogance coming out and come back with a humbler way to respond.

- Start giving praise to team members. Most arrogant leaders have difficulty doing this.

- Work with your leader and ask for help in pointing out situations that could be handled in a more confident and less arrogant manner.

- Listen more. Ask questions. Make more effort to collaborate.

- ***Share credit.***

- Correct others only when it's major, instead of criticizing every little flaw. Use examples of how you overcame something.

I've watched teams with arrogant leaders coming in boasting they are the new sheriff in town, leaders who have outright lied to their staff or placed the blame for their shortcoming onto someone else, and leaders who have stayed holed up in their office sending emails throughout the day. This is the team who wants so badly to create new sales methods, new packages, and have ideas but will never be allowed. Culture quiets down, the team becomes clock watchers, and the room lacks energy and spirit.

I've also watched teams with confident leaders coming in getting to know their team one by one, admitting to mistakes, holding meetings and listening instead of talking, continually inviting the team to help create packages and new ideas, and being present with their team. This is the team atmosphere where you can feel the spirit when you walk in, that has a "can-do" attitude, and has continual energy in the room. They are not clock watchers and will often comment, "I didn't realize it was that late."

Culture starts with the leader. Are you arrogant or confident?

THE NINTH CHIP

COUNSELING OTHERS

One of the most uncomfortable things young leaders find themselves having to do is counselling a team member whose behavior/actions need to change. What to say, how to say it, how will it be received—all of these things play on the mind of a leader. What we need to remember is that our counselling is meant to help change the behavior of the person for the better and for their success. It should not be viewed as a punishment but rather a helping opportunity to become a valuable asset to the organization.

For those of us leaders with kids, we are always careful as parents to remind our children that it is their *actions or behaviors* we are not happy with; not them personally. The *actions or behaviors* needs to change. We still love them, but we don't love their behavior.

It's the same thing in counselling a team member.

We are not saying we don't like them as a person. What we need to change is their behavior or actions in order to continue to be a good fit for the organization. How do we do this?

- **Write down the reason(s) for this discussion**. Which are action/behavior related and which are personal? Remove the personal and focus on the action/behavior-related items. Sometimes it crosses over. For instance, someone is unnecessarily sarcastic to their teammates. This is part of their personality; however, this action can be channeled in a more positive way. In counselling this team member, we would want to have them focus on the delivery of their message.

- **Open the session with an explanation of why you are meeting**. "I set this meeting today to talk to you about the relationship between your goal and the revenue to date that you have brought in." Or, "I set this meeting today to talk to you about the relationship responses you have to your teammates during the course of the day."

- **Be factual.** "I have pulled the past 6 months of revenue to goals and let's look at them together. You are at ___% overall, when the expectation at this point in time is to be at ___%." Or, "I have seen instances which I've jotted down here in which your responses to your teammates has come across negative. For instance, _____. What ways can you see that interpreted by your teammates?"

- **Never compare to others in the room.** This is a one on one with them. It's not about anyone else. The focus is on their actions.

- **Create a measurable plan.** Over the course of the next 30 (or 60) days, here is what will need to be done. List the plan clearly. Make sure it is measurable. That's easier for performance versus actions. For example, "I want you to pause before responding and give yourself two options to answer. Decide which will be received better by the teammate and choose that one. Keep a journal during this time and we will discuss weekly."

Set the dates of follow up.

There is a fine line between putting most of our energy into working with our non-performers or behavioral people and less energy into continuing the growth of those who are functioning well. We counsel, we meet weekly, but we should not put all of our strength into making them better. This is a job they have to do; we are simply giving them the guidelines to do it. Neglecting the rest of the team during this time does not give us the opportunity to continue growing our performers. Make sure there is a good balance.

Oftentimes, little problems turn into big problems because we are reluctant to meet them head on. Some of us really like harmony and don't like dissension. I was guilty of that myself and really have worked hard to improve on that.

When we counsel someone we give them the opportunity to grow. If behavior/action doesn't change and we have to remove someone, we still give them the opportunity to grow. How can this be?

We used to own some small business haircare salons. I remember once counselling one of my team members three different times about attitude and, finally, the last time, with no changes being attempted on her part, I had to let her go. I was young and it was a most uncomfortable moment for me. She was angry. Of course, it was all my fault.

A couple of years later I saw her at a store and was praying she wouldn't see me. She did, and came right up to me. Expecting to continue the uneasy conversation from two years ago, I was surprised to have her say, "Thank you for letting me go. It's the best thing you could have done. I never wanted to admit it, but although I like doing hair, I really didn't like working with the public. I don't like small talk, I don't like listening to people, I just liked to fix their hair. When you let me go, I was angry. But I found a job instead that I absolutely love—I started a moving company and love the fact that I have an initial meeting with people and then I am left to pack things, stack boxes, and just deal with the job and not with the people. I have never been so happy."

I learned at that moment that letting go means freeing up. You are actually freeing up someone to do something that they will be much better at, something that they will be much happier at.

Surprisingly enough, when you let someone go, the team also feels relieved. They don't feel the undercurrent in the room that was there anymore and respect you for considering all of them instead of just one person.

In counselling, we give the person the opportunity to improve behavior. We are there to help them. The choice is truly theirs.

Potato Chip Trainers

Owning Mistakes: Taking a chance

1. Encourage the team to take a chance, with the understanding that you own that chance and all its ups and downs.

2. Share stories with your staff of times you've taken chances and made mistakes and how you resolved them. Let them know that you are human also.

3. If you've made a mistake, create a plan of how you will attack it, including ownership, acknowledgement, discussion, resolution, options, and letting it go. Follow your plan. Thank your team for supporting you during this time.

Confidence/Arrogance: Practicing humble:

1. Ask a mentor to sit in on some meetings and evaluate after.

2. Are you displaying arrogant tendencies? Have them point them out to you.

3. Create a plan for change, share with your mentor, and put it into action, getting feedback from your mentor.

4. Daily: If there is praise to be given to a member of your team, give praise.

5. Before giving a new directive, ask yourself: Is this something that could be a team collaboration?

6. If so, call the team together, explain the outcome you are looking for, and ask them to create the path to get to the outcome.

7. Prior to success stories to your supervisor or others in the organization, list who was responsible along the way to that success.

8. When presenting, include these people for their contributions.

Counselling:

1. Write down the problem as you see it. Define the actions/behavior to change and take away the personal portion.

2. List ways that are measurable to create the change. Make sure that it all focuses on the actions/behavior and isn't personal.

3. Connect with HR prior to presenting to make sure that you are focusing on changing behavior and running through how you will present.

The Tenth
Potato Chip

STRATEGIC LEADING

If we walk out our office door, get into our car, and get a message to drive to Canada, do we know where to start with a plan? How can we go from one season to the next without a clear path of where we are going, how we will get there, the fuel it will take, and the rerouting that may need to happen? This GPS is our strategy.

In talking with staff members from various teams, I find the one thing they are all asking for is structure. There are teams who still use the "fly by the seat of their pants" mentality, teams who use the "react" mentality, and teams that use the "game by game" mentality. There are also teams who have some plans in place for the long term. And there are teams who have a 5-year strategy well planned out, with an overall strategy for each quarter. The latter are the teams that are focused, hitting goals, and having little staff turnover.

They are on a mission, as they have structure.

What is strategy other than a buzzword? Strategy is the overall high-level plan to achieve goals that may or may not happen. We need strategy as it provides a sense of direction for all of us and outlines goals. It helps with decision making and planning. It also enables us to evaluate where we are going and what approaches need to be changed. When we have an overall strategy, we can continue to work with our team on the process to achieve that strategy.

As leaders, we are asked to write our department strategy for obtaining revenue for the upcoming year. Sometimes this is straightforward, sometimes it requires additional hiring or creating another sub-department, and sometimes it requires a structural change within the department. Strategy needs to be well thought out, so it isn't written in an afternoon. It's the notes you take all year as to what will improve the department. It's the changes your staff has suggested that will move the organization forward.

So how do we do this? We create our GPS for the year:

Mission statement. *Why are we going there?* How does your departmental mission statement for the year fit into the organizational mission statement?

Where have you been and where are you to date? *What has been our experience in our travels?* This is crucial in developing strategy. This is actually the focus of the first out-of-season meeting you should have with your team. This helps the sales team understand their part of the puzzle and makes it easier for them to write their strategy and process. Reviewing where the sales have been the past 5 years or so, where changes have occurred, and why will help you determine a realistic approach for the strategy

Identify customer profiles. *Where are the perfect places to go to?* Who is your current ideal customer? Who is a target you are trying to gain? For example, you may be strong in consumer-based season memberships but lack the business numbers that would make sense. This may be a huge target push for you this year. You may want to include more of the thirtysomething age group in memberships and will need to make that a focus.

A SWOT analysis is important. *What are the potential ups and downs on our trip?* What are our strengths as a company/department? What are our team members' assets? What processes did we do that were successful? On the flip side, what processes need improvement? Are there gaps that need to be filled? What would we need that we are missing? What do our customers think of us? Are we confident that our market is growing and people will be buying more or are we stagnating and need changes? Have our members' attitudes toward us changed? Are there competitors to our entertainment in the market now?

Meet with marketing and create a marketing/sales strategy. *What are the best ways to bring others along on our journey?* Review social media and websites and analyze what worked/didn't, influencing words that worked, campaigns that were strong, and those that were weak. Create a plan for timing and introduction of rolling out sales campaigns.

What is going to be your team's strategy to prospect? *How will we get there?* Power hours? Categories? Defining markets? Where are each member's strengths? What would they work best at? What will be the process to work through the pipeline to anticipate closing ratios?

What is your team's strategy to capture a new demographic? *Where can we find someone else to add to our journey?* How will they approach?

Create revenue goals. *What is our timeframe and the cost we anticipate to get there?* There is nothing worse than unrealistic goals and trying to encourage a staff to hit them. I experienced this at one point and, while trying to be a "rah-rah, we can do it leader," my staff is looking at me saying there's no way. And they had valid reasons. They were right and I should have fought for a realistic approach. Stand up for what you believe is realistic. Yes, you can stretch it, but it needs to be attainable and not pie in the sky. Create your revenue goals per staff member. This is not a blanket "divide by x number of people." Set your people up for success. A 4-year veteran and a 1-year member are not at the same sales level. Set a goal for each and, once attained, set a bonus for the next level. In that way, we are not setting goal/stretch goal for the team that they don't get, but rather goal/hit/win and then keep going/bonus!

Team Strategy/Process. *Ask for help along the journey … what will they offer?* This is delivered by your team members to you and to your supervisor (VP). This is their business plan overall to achieve the goals you are setting forth in your strategy. As each member writes their yearly strategy (the who/how/why/when/where/what) they will then zero in each quarter to create the more detailed process they will be using.

Changes needed. *How can I change the journey to make sure it is going to be the most efficient?* In order to accomplish what you want to accomplish in this strategy, what will you need to change? Software? New social media app? Additional staff?

A new department? A change in structure? Many teams are switching to season sellers and group/hospitality sellers and service/retention and finding this far more effective. Why? Few salespeople love selling a full menu. Most are better at one area or another. There are those who are stellar at the instant gratification of a season sale but dread the long-drawn-out process of groups. And there are those who enjoy creating an event and like the long-term planning that a group or hospitality event gives us. Letting them go after what they do best often, after the first year of change, creates success in revenue.

Create your budget. *How much will the journey cost?* Knowing what you need, now create the budget to accomplish it.

The timeline. *When will I reach each milepost along the way?* Do I have a clear outline of the timeline for each strategy and process that I can hold myself and the department accountable to?

The key to strategy writing is CLARITY:

1. Clear measurable outcomes

2. Clear priorities for the upcoming year that the team will focus on

3. Clear steps everyone can follow

4. Clear goals that the team can focus on

Before you take this trip into the next year, make sure you have your GPS clearly defined, you are fueled and ready, your team is in top condition, and you are packed with all the tools you need and ready to go. THIS is your strategy!

THE TENTH CHIP

TRUST THE PROCESS

If strategy is the overall plan, then how do we get to the actual action items? We do this by creating a process. This is where your team comes in and where you often need to do the most coaching.

The days of "pick up phone, call, close, move on" are over. There needs to be a plan in place (strategy) and then the steps (process). Process is a series of actions that gets us to fulfill the goal at hand. We can have the best strategy, but without each and every member having a process in place to make it happen, it won't happen.

As a leader, you have a management process to fulfill. For instance, this would be maximizing the team's time to fulfill the goals at hand. The process might include restructuring staff, hiring additional, breaking down goals into daily versus monthly, offering resources where needed, etc. It can also be availability for meetings with the team member and a client, a quicker decision-making process, etc. Figuring out your part of the process is key to helping the staff manage theirs.

The next step is helping your team create their process. When breaking a strategy down to quarters (here is the revenue needed this quarter, what should be the focus during this quarter), the next step for the team will be deciding the process to accomplish the focus and revenue for that quarter. Helping them manage this is instrumental to your coaching and their growth.

How do you help your team create their process? It's the who, what, when, where, why and how of planning their sales.

1. **Who** will be their target market? This may be drafting categories of businesses or groups, a specific demographic they may want to go after, etc. For instance, one team member wanted to focus on small businesses. Another wanted to focus on large businesses. Another wanted to focus on non-profits. Who do they want to build relationships with? This is the prospecting phase and is crucial to your team's success. Teach prospecting. Encourage prospecting hours in their day.

2. **What** can you find out about your prospect before you even make the call? What will connect you to that person faster? Asking for someone specifically rather than, "Who might you connect me with that ___" is a big step over a hurdle. The prework you do sets you up for success. Teach your team that knowledge is a powerful thing.

3. **Where** is your target market? Will you own a city? Will you focus on a region ? A zip code? Where can you go to prospect? Where can you go to find "like people" that buy from us? Where can you best spend your time?

4. **When** is the best time to reach categories so that the team structures their power hours logically? For instances, business calls generally work better in the morning. Calling groups and organizations and consumers is better in the later afternoon. Help your team learn to know their market and how to best maximize their time.

5. **Why** do they believe certain categories are better than other? Why do they want to go after a specific category? Can they create a solid plan around it?

6. **How** will they connect? How will they present? Preparation is key. Are there packages they want to create? They need to have it all ready before the first call.

The whole point of this is, how will your team hold themselves accountable and what will be their plan of attack for the quarter? How will they structure their day? As part of their process, they should plan to send you a weekly process that fits into their quarterly. Each evening, before they leave, they should have a sheet on their desk with their prospects for the two power hours and their plan by half hour for the next day. This structure enables them to stay focused on the process they put together and makes it easier for you to coach them.

Now how do you best help and coach your team through this process?

As a leader, you need to analyze the current sales process and identify changes that need to be made. Suggest this to your team so they can make the adjustments needed for success.

Next, it's important as their leader that you assess them as they go through this process. After they've written it and you've finetuned it, assess them as they are doing it. Are there changes that need to be made in the presentation? For instance, I find reps create the process and get excited but forget the most important thing is talk time. They are in a hurry to either close or set a meeting without establishing needs or having true conversations. Help your reps see the steps they took to get through this process. It's called process for a reason.

As you assess, recognize what it took in the process to get from prospect to yes. Were there objections to overcome? Were there examples to be given? Were there in-person visits needed? Following up with email? How many calls? All of this can be documented for each sale and the rep will begin to see their process really unfold. At this point, you can identify steps that would make the process more efficient or easier for the rep.

Help the reps identify each step in their process. With that, identify what they need in each step so that they are prepared ahead of time and can function with more confidence.

Your role as leader is to coach your team. Their day-to-day process that they put together is the most important thing they will do to create success. Your guidance in this process enables you to coach the members to successfully hit goals. The more you help them with this process and the better they get, the more confidence they will acquire. And now their discussions with prospects will become so much stronger, and instead of a sales "pitch," your team will now be doing a sales "presentation through conversation."

POTATO CHIP LEADERSHIP SKILLS

SAMPLE STRATEGY/PROCESS

Goals:

- $____ = goal for groups

- Goal for November-January = $___ in group bowl/hospitality

- Revenue as a group sales department - November-January $___

- Hit at least $___ a week in group deposits or full payments

- Spend an hour minimum each day prospecting to help get more prospects in the pipeline

- Take time specifically in November and December to follow up with season ticket holders who haven't renewed, invite season ticket holders to renewal party on ___

- Follow up again with them after the holidays to let them know they should renew ASAP

- Take time to invite out all retirement homes from last season's Senior Day to attend this year's senior day

- Invite retirement homes who were not able to come this past season

- Go to as many senior networking events as possible to promote senior day

- Focus on Volunteer Appreciation Day in the upcoming season: get to a minimum of 20 groups, companies, and organizations that use volunteers weekly to explain the event and the deposit for a space

- Own a city and spend 1 full day a week in that city meeting businesses, organizations, and churches

- Renew at least two big hospitality groups by the beginning of January

Processes: New Business Techniques

1. What techniques will you use to acquire the new business?

2. What will be your routes to gatekeepers/influencers/strategic partners; others who can/will collaborate with you to develop your market; what would be in it for them?

3. Sales plan: what is the product you want to focus on/value/segment/whatever is relevant?

4. How will you get to this goal? In person? Hosting events? Attending meetings/events? A unique twist to capture attention? Different way to sell existing product? Influencers? Libraries?

5. What will be unique for you to try this year? Get out of your comfort zone and use a different technique.

Pipelines:

1. How will you build your pipeline to include cold (new), warm (working with them), hot (will close shortly), remove for future (remember: to hit your goal you MUST have a minimum of 3x the amount in your pipeline

2. Plan for keeping pipeline current throughout year ... a closed deal means you have one less prospect.

Call volumes/power hours/appointments:

1. Goal for day/week for calls–

2. Number of new clients per week you will get an appointment with

3. Setting a power hour twice a day to get appointments set, introduce yourself, etc. Your plan per week for closing.

POTATO CHIP LEADERSHIP SKILLS

Prospecting:

1. How do you plan on new prospecting?

2. How will you create new business?

3. Where will you find "our" people?

4. How will you introduce new people to our product? (ex, large businesses, small businesses)

Events:

1. Events you feel you should attend on a monthly basis to be where "our people" are, working/attending events that focus on who our clients are.

Out-of-office canvassing:

1. How often will you do this?

2. How will you pick clients/locations to stop in?

3. How will you track?

4. Will you own a city? Which one? HOW?

Social media:

1. How can you use to your advantage?

2. Using LinkedIn intelligently not just to post and hope to sell.

3. Who are your contacts in the area looking at? Who are their contacts?

4. You should be inviting every contact you meet to connect through LinkedIn so you can see more people/companies like them.

Your supervisor/mentor:

1. Where/when/how do you see their need for assistance?

Segments:

1. Who do you see as your segment? Have you researched your CRM or sales database to understand who your best customer is?

2. Where do you find your challenges with these segments?

Set Your Daily Business Schedule:

1. Daily timeline of what day will look like.

2. Include power hours, focus calls, call volume, appointments.

3. Schedule your day, knowing it may change—but overall how will you strategize your day?

Accountability:

1. How will you hold yourself accountable weekly? What measure?

2. Revenue

3. Call volume

4. Appointments

5. Canvassing

6. Owning a city

7. Asking for help

POTATO CHIP LEADERSHIP SKILLS

Personal Goal Side:

1. Define what you believe are your strongest assets and where you need to grow to get to the next level.

2. Explain reasons that you feel hold you back from getting to the next level.

3. Pick 2 key areas you would like to grow in this year to make it to the next level of your career.

4. Define what you plan to do to grow in those 2 areas and how you will evaluate success in accomplishing this.

Potato Chip Trainers

Plan for a mid-season SWOT analysis.

Use this as to energize the team mid-season.

List:

1. What is working and to what degree of success?

2. What has not been working and needs to be changed?

3. Is it the idea or the process? If the idea, change it. If the process, have the team decide how to change the process in the second half to make it successful.

Review your current departmental strategy:

1. What is missing?

2. What needs to be enhanced?

3. Does it tell the story of how we will improve this year to hit the goals?

4. Is there a measurable plan?

5. Is it clear?

6. Meet with each team member and ask them to review for you what the plan was for this season. Was the messaging clear and concise enough to be heard by the team?

7. Are there specific processes built out?

8. Is there a timeline created with it that's clearly defined?

POTATO CHIP LEADERSHIP SKILLS

Have the team create a team strategy and a personal business plan for the quarter:

1. Focusing on the next 3 months, have the team brainstorm as to what is most important to generate revenue during that time.

2. Decide on two to three actionable items.

3. Create a timeline with them.

4. Based on the actionable items, have each rep write their personal business plan for the quarter, which includes the who/how/what/when/where/why as well as their overall daily schedule.

5. Have them present their personal business strategies to you and your supervisor.

6. Hold them accountable to this strategy.

The Eleventh
Potato Chip

WHAT WOULD STAFF SAY ABOUT YOU AS A LEADER?

Moving across country after a million years in one spot is no easy feat! Going through volumes of saved stuff is even worse. One good thing … some of it brings back great memories and helps me remember how I was, how I changed, and where I still need to be.

One of the things I found during a recent move was a letter written by my staff when I was leaving nursing. At the time, it meant a lot sentimentally. Right now, it means volumes more, because now I realize the letter pretty much sums up what leadership should be if we want followers.

Here are some of the attributes they shared that they felt I displayed. These hold steadfast no matter the career you are in:

Fair, honest, and loyal. This is what every staff wants above all else. Be fair with all of them, don't play favorites, and what's good for one is good for another. Honesty is crucial … no telling white lies just to get yourself off the hook. Admitting errors, admitting you don't know something … all this strengthens the respect. Loyalty, both to the organization AND to the staff, speaks more than words.

*Calm, capable, and quietly efficient, even under stress…*constantly laboring for more efficiency, better and more equitable working conditions…these are things that were mentioned. How often do you stand up for your staff when you feel they deserve better? Or do you simply feel "it's the rule." Sometimes, we have to show upper management that things are changing, and we must change with them. What happens when we get a little "beat up" by upper management? Do we take it out on our staff? Are we screamers, intimidators, feared, or do we put aside those feelings and maintain that consistency that all staff members hope for? Remember, stress is contagious. Don't make your problem their problem.

Available for problems large or small with the assurance that you will listen and help if possible ... great communication. Do we ignore problems hoping they go away or listen? Do we give double talk or truly listen and help them move forward? As the note said, "coworkers were willing to happily exert themselves above and beyond ordinary limits in times of stress and heavy work load, because she also did and understood us." Do you tell your staff to do stuff or do you walk the walk, talk the talk? If you head sales, do you still sell? Do you handle complaints or just let the service staff do it?

Not above soiling your hands to help at stressful or busy times. Do we "tell" or help "do?" Do we help lighten the load, letting the staff know we are in this together? Do we maintain a good temper, a smile, and give a lift to our team's day? During renewals, do we pitch in and help renew the difficult ones or tell your staff it needs to be done? During prime sales contests, do we join a contest and help sell also? Do we believe everyone sells and everyone services?

As I read their letter, it not only brought tears to my eye but also made me realize that some things don't change in life. Things like: Common courtesy. Honesty. Integrity. Caring. Communicating. Helping. Listening. Calmness. Consistency. Motivation. Fairness. Honesty. Loyalty. Don't ask others to do what you wouldn't do. Leave your problems at home. Bring a smile and positive attitude to the day. The ability to forgive and forget. The ability to believe in your people. Give them every opportunity to succeed.

It's easy to say, "Treat others the way you want to be treated." But how often, as we move up the corporate ladder, do we remember that? We tend to fall into place and act how we are "supposed" to act.

What would YOUR staff say about your leadership actions? Are you leading, managing, or intimidating? Are you moving your staff forward or holding them back from true success? Are they selling/servicing by fear or by belief? This letter was a true reflection of what a staff values in leadership. How do we hold up to those standards?

ENGAGEMENT COACHING METHODS

Happy customers = happy business owners. Sports teams, large businesses, small businesses … all of us want our customers to be engaged and singing our praises. But it doesn't happen with a purchase. It doesn't even necessarily happen with a winning sports team. But it does happen if your own company culture is engaged.

If you want your organization to be on the top of the success ladder, it starts with you:

Learn your own strengths. Learn how you interact with others in the organization. Learn what kind of influencer you are and what kind of leader you are.

From there, **learn about your staff's strengths**. Learn how to better interact with them. Learn how to maximize their efforts through their strengths.

Next, **engage your staff members one by one**. Understand their job. Listen. Learn their strengths and let them excel and bring ideas to the table. Don't let them be caretakers of your ideas … let them create ideas and execute them.

Coach your team for engagement. Team meetings should be highly engaged … ideas exchanged … goals set by the members … how they will be measured set by the members. When it comes from them, it will be hard to fail. No one wants their ideas to fail—the extra hours, the commitment, the determination—it will all be fired up!

Coaching 1:1 based on engagement: Have them set their goals for the next few weeks in the coaching session and decide how they will measure. You will have far less goals missed and far more excited staff members. Don't wait for quarterly/ yearly evaluations. Coaching should be done weekly or biweekly if you want to have an engaging team.

Change culture? It's already changing if you are doing all of the above. You will have staff arriving early, staying late, excited, celebrating victories, eager to come up with more ideas. This is a team that functions with "buzz" whether you are in the room or not. This is a team that is constantly on the go, looking for that next sale, knowing what it takes to get the job done. This is a team that doesn't wait for instruction; instead, they plan their strategy.

And then what happens? This spills over to the customer. You can have a well-trained service team, but unless they are engaged and in an engaging culture, the customer will never feel it. We engage the customer when our staff is engaged. Passion, enthusiasm, concern, support … it's all there when your team is part of an engaged culture. Best of all, your customer retention goes up, whether there's a new team in town or a new competitive business in town. The customer will be loyal as they feel part of the company. Pricing won't be a concern, perks won't be a concern. What your customer knows is this: The staff is happy to be there, the staff is happy the client is there, and the staff makes sure the client is part of the business.

And that is a WIN in everyone's book!

BUILDING YOUR TEAM EFFECTIVELY

For those of you who stay up late and watch the old reruns of *I Love Lucy*, you will remember the classic commercial she made for "Vitameatavegamin."

In it, after having a few too many sips of the tonic, she asks, "Are you tired? Rundown? Listless? Do you poop out at parties? Are you unpopular? Well, are you?"

We all laugh at it, but we need to ask ourselves the same questions. Does your team lack motivation? Seem spiritless in meetings? Call off frequently? Clock watch? Does making coffee each day get more interest than a new idea? Do fantasy sports teams have more effort put into them than the job at hand? Do they poop out by 2:00, ready for a nap?

If so, your team is functioning with the 9 to 5, "it's a job," "my work has no value," "my happiness starts at 5," mentality. There is no buy-in to company values and mission statement. "Development" is seen as a word and not as an achievable action. You are left with a team that will not rise to the occasion of creating a workable plan, let alone go through walls for you. You find yourself frustrated, looking for that new "best hire" who will make everyone else's game come up a notch.

But wait—you are your *own* best hire! The answer isn't necessarily continually trying to find that new best hire but rather looking at yourself.

How to get everyone on board with where you want them to go?

Step 1: Invite your team to create the future

Call your team together and have open conversations about what everyone feels they can/should achieve for the good of the organization and department in 3 months/6 months/1 year/3 years. Ask them to set project goals. Put your department mission statement together collectively. Live it. Breathe it. They are a part of this company. They need to know the vision of the company. They need to create their own vision to fulfill that objective. That helps create buy-in. They are not simply "selling to make the company rich." They are selling perhaps to redesign an area of the facility, to redesign premium areas, etc. They need to know what they are working toward, then they can create the vision each year to get them there.

Step 2: Focus

Ask the team to create and write down the action steps to achieve this future. Now look at your team and each of their individual strengths. Invite them to utilize their strengths to build on these action steps. In essence, let them create the future based on where they best excel. Everyone's strengths contribute to the sum of the whole. Let them know their strengths are valued and important to the organization and to the team's ability to achieve their future.

Everyone should walk away with a solid purpose and individual plan, as well as a spring in their step as they realize they are being called upon to excel in areas they feel they *can* excel in. You have set the stage for success and confidence.

Step 3: Engage with the team daily with positive energy

As the saying goes, "feed the positive dog." Having been a nurse, we always said energy is muscle … the more it's used, the stronger it gets. Get out of the office. Walk around and be part of your team.

Focus.

Focus on the vision.

Focus on the goals the team has set. Stop and talk to them individually as to how they are achieving their portion of that goal. Genuinely listen and have a conversation. Show interest. Get excited. Give support. People thrive on positive energy. When you are enthusiastic and feel genuinely interested and excited, everyone does. Leave them a note or an afterhours voicemail for a job well done.

Step 4: Give them ownership of the goals and projects they set

When it's *your* idea and *your* project, you tend to take personal pride and ownership and don't want it to fail. You become more team oriented to make sure it works, collaborating with others and doing more research and brainstorming than when assignments are doled out. It may be easier to be authoritative and assign, but if you want the team firing on all cylinders with excitement, energy, and a desire to achieve, give them ownership. Let them create the ideas, the projects, and the strategy under your guidance.

Step 5: Coach your team 1:1 based on their strengths, business strategy, and personal accountability

Have them write their own business strategy, along with timetables, for the goals. Coach them based on their strengths and their strategy to help them achieve their goals. Hold them accountable, but help them through rough times if needed, based on what they themselves set for accountability. The buck stops with the person who created the goal … themselves. They must be accountable but need that coaching and help when roadblocks arrive to achieve.

Step 6: Celebrate success

All too often, we only celebrate quarterly or yearly, if at all. Celebrate after goals are achieved. Just like kids, punishment/reward too long after the fact loses meaning. Celebrate as a team when success is achieved. Let them feel great before embarking on the next goal/project. All too often we stop sharing the excitement. A new rep will come in and say they get embarrassed to celebrate so we stop. We don't ring a bell. We don't send out our e-chain. We don't have fun. The product on the field or court or ice celebrates a basket, a run, a goal. That is what a team is. They don't hit a home run and sit down quietly in the dugout. They don't get a touchdown and quietly get back in formation. They celebrate. If the product we are working for does it, why aren't we creating that same team atmosphere in the office?

Let's keep your team from pooping out at 2:00, being spiritless in meetings, and having the highlight of their day be a new pot of coffee or energy drink. You CAN create a happily motivated team!

THE ELEVENTH CHIP

WHAT IS YOUR WORK OBITUARY?

"So live that when you die, the poor, the sick, the lonely, will mourn the passing of a friend." So was the life of Veronica Sogan Tokarczyk, 94, of Lorain, Ohio.

Born in a coal mining town of West Virginia, Veronica moved at a young age to Lorain, where she lived her entire life. A woman who took great pride in being a grandmother, great-grandmother, great-great grandmother, and friend, Veronica was not one to worry about material things but rather making sure others had what they needed.

Besides her family, Veronica was a nurturer who loved God's earth and was an avid gardener, living most of her years from the fresh fruits and vegetables of her garden; crocheter, making beautiful things for family and friends and winning many awards at the Lorain County Fair; a woman who could make any unusual plant grow, blossom, and bear fruit. She loved mowing her lawn. Above all, she believed in giving the best of herself to everyone she met and would share whatever she had if someone was in need.

She is survived by what she considered her greatest accomplishments, her children Joseph Tokarczyk, Jim Tokarczyk, Judy Balzer, and Kathy Burrows; 10 grandchildren, 14 great-grandchildren, one great-great-grandchild, wonderful neighbors, who have been most kind to her, and wonderful friends who brought her much joy.

In the spirit of mom's love to give, we ask that you remember someone less fortunate in her name.

You are probably wondering why I included this obituary in my book. What would you say about this remarkable woman, who happened to be my mother? What type of life did she live? What do you think the comments from friends, neighbors, and people we didn't even know were like?

This was a story of a life well lived, a life that was spent in helping others become the best they could be while still enjoying the woman she was.

If you were to leave your job today and your staff wrote your work obituary, what would they say about you? Be honest. None of us like to think that others just may not "like our style," but fact is, more often than not, many on the team will not feel any impact on your leaving or staying, let alone say that we are dictatorial, close minded, difficult to work for, a poor communicator, etc. If you are having a positive impact and the staff truly looks at you as an open-minded person who encourages strengths and individualization versus one size fits all, respects the ideas of many versus only of themselves, and lets us "use our brain" versus mind-numbing groupthink, then kudos to you! But what about the rest of us?

I often use this tactic in my coaching for leadership workshops, and people don't always want to be very honest as to how they are perceived. Seeing ourselves as others see us is a tremendous first step to becoming better leaders. It gives us the opportunity to change our way of thinking/leading, and create teams that feel committed, passionate, and creative.

I remember once during a long-term consulting role when one of the team members said to me, "You really don't like conflict do you?" I was taken aback for a moment and then realized, that's right, I don't. I may not like it but how I handle it is important. Obviously, I wasn't handling it in the best way possible. This opened me up to learning how to be better at this. If this is how I am perceived, then it's something that needs changing. I was so appreciative of that comment, as it enabled me to grow.

What are some of the comments you have had? Have you ignored them, been upset, written them off as from a grumpy staff or sat down and seriously looked at yourself and how you can change that for the better?

As a leader, what do you want others to say about you? What would be your legacy to your team and your organization?

How can we do this? Let's take an in-depth look at ourselves:

What has changed since I've started working here? Has it been for the better or the worse? Can I name three improvements that the staff would say I've brought, not just what I think I've improved?

What has changed in the way we look at problems? Am I approaching as a team with new ideas or do I resort to what I've always done?

What has changed in the way I approach staff? Is it for the better? Is communication open? Do I do more listening and less talking?

What would my staff do differently because they've worked with me? Am I leaving a positive legacy of growth and development?

What do they think about differently since I've been here? Do they simply make calls or do they have ownership of their own business and host their own meetings?

What would they emulate from you? What have you given of the best of yourself that they can emulate? Have you given the best of yourself?

In what regard might they say, "I'm never going to be like him/her"? What are your less desirable traits that the staff picks up on?

What lasting impact have you created on the organization? On the staff? Is it positive? Is it worth repeating? Can you be proud of it?

Let's get YOUR work obituary looking good! Make sure you are leaving a great impact on how a team should be run and creating a staff with a "can-do," energetic, and passionate attitude. Find great leaders as mentors to help you in being a role model just as I do, as I want MY work obituary to continue to be written by a staff that is now energized, happy, passionate, and growing!

TRAVEL GUIDE > TOUR GUIDE

One of the biggest myths is that a leader should be the one who sells the most, talks the loudest, and is the biggest producer. It's who everyone considers the cream of the crop. But is that really leadership? Oftentimes, we take our best salesperson and move them up to a managerial role, don't coach them, and fail to give them tools to grow. We tend to wind them up and let them run.

What we have done is failed them. They are out of their role where they did so well and, without coaching and guidance, we have set them up to become frustrated, unhappy in their job, and wondering where they failed. We need to bring our potential leaders along with us on the journey … not just wind them up and expect them to function. We need to find who our tour guides are and develop them.

Work is a journey. Leaders take people with them on this journey. You don't go by yourself. To lead, you must have followers. You must have people you are working with, not over.

A tour guide or a travel agent. What is the difference? The travel agent gives you brochures and tells you about the trip, but they may or may not have been there. They get the tickets, plan the hotel, give you an itinerary, and send you on your way. An important job, but just one step in the process. This is the way some leaders are … travel agents. They send out an announcement, tell you what you need to do, expect it done their way, but don't follow it through. You can't use your brain and see what more you can achieve, tap other resources, or be coached along the journey. Travel agent leaders are more authoritative. Is this what you want? Are you sending someone where you've never been simply by telling them what you want done? Is the communication short lived? "Go out and do this."

Great travel agents will set you up with a tour guide. Inspirational leader tour guides. These are the leaders who inspire their staff to use their brain, stopping to appreciate where they are along the way. They say, "Let me show you something. I'm going to take you places where I've been and lived and tell you all about them as we go along. I'm going to let you in on the journey." This is the type of leader whose staff will move mountains for them and the company. They are brought along the journey and shown opportunities they never dreamed of. And they are given mentoring and coaching along the way.

Why are some lonely at the top? You can't be leading if no one is following. Get off the mountain and bring the team or your younger leaders with you. Coach your team or new leaders through this journey. Don't send them to a faraway island and let them fend for themselves. Let them know you made mistakes, too. Share with them how you learned, who inspired you, who didn't inspire you. Review some of the things they've done and ask what they've learned and how could they do it even better next time. You're on this journey together. Encourage your people and make them feel like winners.

Welcome tour guides of the business world! See, share, and bring others along with you. Notice qualities you like in others that inspire you and make them one of your qualities. See qualities that you don't like in others and know that is someone you don't want to emulate. You don't need a title to make your mark. You need only to bring others along on the journey. Coaching. Inspiration. Motivation. Leaders. Tour Guides.

POTATO CHIP LEADERSHIP SKILLS

WHAT DO YOU BRING TO THE TEAM AS A LEADER?

What do you stand for? Does the team see inspired, heartfelt leadership or a hurricane that leaves chaos when going through?

What are values and the concepts you can bring to the team and how can you do it?

Vision. There's such a great feeling when everyone is chasing after a larger prize. It's not just a revenue number they are going after. It's what the revenue number stands for. Is it contributing to paying a player? Then let them "own" the player. Upon hitting the goal, can the player meet them? Sign something for them? Appreciate them? Is the achieved goal going to create a difference in the future look of the facility? Let them be part of the groundbreaking. It's so much more than a number … it's being part of the bigger picture. If we can't include the staff in the vision of the organization, there is going to be a lack of loyalty and passion.

Creating buy-in … commitment. Are we committed to our team? Are they committed to us and the organization? Have we taken the steps to build that commitment? Have we defined the goals clearly? Do they know their part in them? Have you relayed the obstacles as you see them so they know that the future is not always rosy and will take work? Have you then relayed to them how you will remove those obstacles so they can move forward? In order to be all in, we have to first "buy in." Openness on your part will help.

Trust. Is your team confident in going to you with questions? Do they get answers in a timely manner? Are you able to make decisions or always double checking? Can you display confidence in them and yourself? Do they believe you believe they can do it? Are you showing them the way?

Involvement. Does every member of your team feel part of the process? Do they feel their thoughts are valuable? Do they feel they are allowed to have a voice? Remember, we as leaders don't have to have all the answers. But we do have to have the ability to incorporate answers by involving others in the process.

Respect. Sing it, Aretha! Respect is earned, not automatically given with a title. How are you earning your respect? How can you better communicate? How can you better follow through? Listen? Include your team? Just like a parent, make "no" mean something. If you say it all the time, it removes all respect and creates a very complacent culture. Earn it and your team will go through a wall for you.

Empowering. When we let go and let others, we empower them. This puts the team more in control of their actions and how they go about attaining their goals, as well as growing confidence. In order to empower, we have to loosen control. This is one of the hardest things we do as leaders. Note, I said "loosen." I didn't say give control up. Why? You are still overseeing them. Just like kids, we will keep them from hurting themselves but we will encourage them to experience and learn lessons along the way.

Collaboration. Never add this to your value statement unless you truly plan on doing it. I've experienced teams that have this written in stone, yet it never happens. Consequently, culture quickly erodes. How often do you call the team together to create an idea or plan versus telling them the idea or plan? Are you creating an environment by being collaborative in which everyone wants to come and be a part of it? Do you create team contests where everyone works together toward the goal?

Innovation. Are you able to take "this is the way we've done it" out of your vocabulary? The "if it isn't broke, don't fix it" mentality? That may be true but is the team moving forward and excited or complacent and ho-hum? Encouraging the team to think creatively and asking them how and what they think about things lets them look at you as a leader in a new light. They are using their gray matter … this is most exciting to them. And you are letting them. And listening.

Empathy. What is your commitment to everyone in the room? To each individual? As a great director once told me, "We hold our teams' lives in our hands. We play a big part as to if they can pay rent, if they can make their bills, if they are happy." Do we see them as the individuals they are, and do we commit to growing them the best they can so that they can meet their personal goals, as well as the company goals? Are we professionally concerned about them?

Ownership. One of the quotes I love is "Autograph your work with excellence." We can't do that unless we have ownership of our work. Do we allow our members to take ownership? Ownership is the right of possessing something, so do we let our team own their small business?

It's nice to have a list of values and concepts as part of your visionary statement of your organization. It's great when you, as a leader, make them come alive each and every day with your team.

MANAGEMENT EXAMPLES: BREWING COMPANIES

How often do we see our leaders trying to force culture, speaking in what they feel is a correct, precise manner, creating a rah-rah speech that sounds good but has no heart, but when push comes to shove, they see themselves as doing all they could, but they just don't have the right staff to make it happen?

Great Managers, Directors, VPs, Presidents, and CEOs aren't created by reading the right books, using the right buzz words with the staff, and never seeing themselves as the problem. Great leaders are created by working *alongside* their staff, not *over* their staff.

Take the Manager I experienced at Saddle Mountain Brewing Company in Goodyear, Arizona. Some of my kids came out for the holiday weekend and we decided to have a bite at Saddle Mountain.

We gave our name and was told it would be "a little bit" as they were busy. After waiting for quite a while, I went up and asked how much longer it might be. She then explained they only had one server and so they couldn't put us at the community table but would need to wait until a table for six opened. So again, we waited.

Then out came a gentleman who asked if we needed a table. I explained we were waiting for a table for six for a bit. He promptly said, "Give me two minutes and I will prepare the community table for you and I will personally be your server." Two minutes later, he came over, invited us in, and had menus, silverware, and water waiting for us. He again apologized and took our beverage order and then, returning with those, took our order.

Later, he came over and talked with us a bit. He said that historically, this time last year they were lucky to have five tables filled at a time. Business had been booming and, with it being a holiday weekend, they anticipated it would die down and he didn't schedule as well as he should have. He *apologized to us* for it and said that he couldn't ask the staff to do any more than they were already doing, and so he chose to take us and a few others who came in.

What? A manager who rolls up his sleeves and helps? A manager who apologizes to his staff and client for under scheduling? A manager who was continually asking those working if they needed help with anything and was continually on the floor with them? This gentleman earned my respect as a customer and definitely earned staff respect as their leader. What about us?

POTATO CHIP LEADERSHIP SKILLS

As a leader, think about the times …

- In the box office when the lines are horrendously long and, instead of opening a window and helping, the leader stands back and watches their staff working, ready to "solve a problem" if there is one.

- A customer has been angry and is asking for a manager and, instead of stepping up and taking their call/visit, you tell your staff how to handle them.

- Staff is struggling to hit a goal and instead of sitting down with them, discussing their approach and how we might change it, then being the example by getting on the phone and making some calls of your own to show by leading, you instead belittle them for not hitting it or not trying hard enough.

- As the game is going on and your staff is hustling all over, do you walk around to check on the staff, or sit and watch some of the game, or worse, go back to your office instead of standing with the staff for a bit at the sales table, going with a staff member to visit their groups, helping pass out gifts at the season ticket booth, or stepping into the customer service booth to help a bit?

- The day you became a leader, did you rejoice as you felt you wouldn't have to get on the phones to sell anymore? Or did you realize it was a great opportunity to coach by example?

- Have you insisted on a private office away from the staff? The best leaders are part of their staff. The best leaders *sit among the sales staff,* being an active leader vs a hands-off leader. I have had major league teams where a CEO has his desk right in with the sales team, a VP sits in a cubicle with their sales teams, offices that have every office opening to the sales room so they can all hear and share. These are leaders. I've also had those where their leader sits away from them, behind closed doors, or worse, on another floor.

- Have you ever apologized to your staff for mishandling a situation or do you gloss it over?

- Have you inspired your staff by inviting ideas then acting on them or do you feel you need to inspire by intimidation?

- How often have you asked your staff if they need help and then given it?

- How often have you cared about them as valued employees, with a family and a life outside work, not just the people who bring in your sales?

- How often have you remembered what it was like to be them and what you really liked/didn't like in leaders you had?

- What do you know about your staff?

When you go out into the world and see great leadership in action, it needs to be acknowledged. Unfortunately, in today's rat race, we forget that the only way to achieve success is the value we give to our employees. We show that by actions, not by great speeches.

RETENTION

When it comes to visiting a city, the only way to truly see it is to walk it. For me, it's about seeing it all, which means the nooks, the crannies, and meeting the people. Meeting the locals gives you the fabric and fiber that the city is made of. And that is what I found one night in San Francisco ...

While visiting my kids, we made dinner reservations at a long-established, small Italian restaurant in North Beach called Trattoria Contadina. Arriving early, I sat at the bar to wait for my kids while meeting Vince, the bartender. Being the only person at the bar at that time, I chatted with Vince ... where he was from, how long he had worked there, etc. And what I found was a fascinating story of how businesses should be run.

Trattoria Contadina began with Vince's grandfather and has been in existence under his family for 30 years, with the average time an employee works there being 14 years ... in the restaurant business! He introduced me to the chef who has been there 33 years (before his grandfather bought it), servers who have been there since the day the family opened it, dishwashers who have been there 15 years, and more. This was fascinating to me, in a day and age where those in sports are leaving often after 8 months. What do they attribute to keeping their employees in a business that one would consider high turnover? A few simple reasons I learned that night ...

- *They are family owned but family is a team.* Ideas are generated from the staff themselves and everyone has a say in the business. This is as much their business as it is the family's who owns it.

- *The staff is appreciated.* Just sitting there watching them in action as the restaurant started to fill: team members help each other out, compliments are passed back and forth, "How is your son doing?" etc. Smiles by the staff are genuine here.

- *The staff knows the history of the business.* They don't just work there, they are a part of it. You can ask any of them a question about the business and they will tell you with pride the history, the longevity, and the appreciation they have to be able to work there. Beyond refreshing!

- *They are paid as valued employees.* Simply put, if your staff is good and you want them to stay, pay them what they are worth. They make a living at this job, and because of that are more than willing to stay.

- *No one is better than another.* Vince didn't just wait for a server to pick up the drinks ordered … if he was free, he took them to the table himself. If a server was free, they assisted another. They worked as a team, not as individuals.

- *It starts at the top.* The owner is there nightly, managing the reservations, talking with and helping staff, mingling with customers and staff alike—not isolated in an office, creating what they think is the next best idea, but rather mingling with both customers and staff getting a realistic feel for the pulse.

How frustrating is it to a sports client to call their rep only to find year after year they have a different one due to turnover? What does that say about you as an organization?

Coming from a sports world of turnover, frustration, and 1980s mentality, it was refreshing to see one of the most challenging businesses to own have their magic formula down pat to keeping a loyal staff. Without question, it starts at the top. Does yours? Are you leading in a way that invites your team to stay or rather beat the door down?

Potato Chip Trainers

Improve stress management.

1. Write down every stress-filled engagement you had the past week.

2. What was your reaction?

3. How did the staff react to how you handled your stress?

4. What results would you rather have?

5. Create three steps you will now use when a stressful situation occurs so as to handle it in a calm, logical manner.

Improve problem solving.

1. Write the problem down.

2. Make two columns.

3. Create two ways to handle the problem, writing one in each column.

4. Write the potential outcome and objections with each method.

5. Choose the stronger one.

Improve team engagement.

1. Write down a list of three goals for the upcoming month you as a team have to achieve

2. Call together a Breakfast of Champions: a morning breakfast meeting with the team, complete with Wheaties, OJ, pastries, etc.

3. List the three goals.

4. As champions, ask them which goal as a team they would like to help you with cracking the code.

5. Once decided, have the team brainstorm ideas as to how they can best achieve that goal in the next month.

6. Give them full ownership from marketing the ideas to creating the wording to the way they want to "sell" the goal.

7. Tell them you will have weekly check-in breakfast and pastries as to the achievement toward the goals, as you are eager to hear/see their results.

Create the future with your team.

1. This is great for the end-of-the-season/start-of-the-new-season kickoff.

2. Present to the team the vision for the year: revenue, retention, touch points, etc.

3. Ask the team to create a how-to guide as to accomplish this.

4. Once the guide has been posted, identify what your role as leader will be in each section.

5. Create contracts: a sales team contract and a leader contract listing each of your commitments you have just made. Sign and distribute to all.

Create your work obituary based on the questions in the article.

1. Once written, highlight those needing improvement.

2. Put together a personal strategy for improvement on each item.

The Twelfth
Potato Chip

THE BOSS PEOPLE WANT TO WORK FOR

Having mentored and coached staff members, leaders, and developing leaders across the country, I have heard many common requests when it comes to leadership.

Below are the top ten most repeated wishes that staff ask for:

#10: Welcome us when we start. Whether an email, a note, a voicemail left, or a personal visit. Let us know that you are happy about us joining the team, confirming in our mind that we made the right decision.

I once knew a boss that scheduled 15 minutes with every new employee the first week of their hire.

#9: Empower us and let us have ownership of projects. Let us feel engaged with the company. If we feel engaged, hours don't matter, projects don't matter, we are "all in."

I have known bosses who are interested enough to check in on members when working on projects and see how they are progressing, encouraging along the way. The staff is happy, energized, and is not afraid to spend an evening when needed.

#8: Understand and respect that we have homes, apartments, significant others, children, and obligations outside of work. Please don't make comments or suggestions of what I have/don't have, how I should join the local golf club as the membership is "cheap," where I should/do shop … understand that we are probably on an entirely different level so we need to ensure mutual respect. Please know that

I really do want to get home prior to my spouse/children going to bed or eating dinner without me.

I have known bosses who stay late and get angry and make remarks when a staff member leaves at 7 (day ends at 5), failing to realize that perhaps that staff member would like to see their child before they go to bed or have a nice family dinner before homework and bed.

#7: Acknowledge accomplishments that I or my teammates achieve. We get so excited when we know you care. Walk around the office and acknowledge us, know who we are, know a little about us.

One of the best leaders I have had the honor of knowing is not afraid to manage by walking around and can be found in most any department talking with staff, acknowledging them in person for an achievement.

#6: Care about me as a person, not just as a worker in the company. I have hobbies, interests, outside talents. We may find common bonds.

One of the best leadership moments is sending a note/gift card to the spouse of an employee before an extremely busy/stressful time, letting them know that you recognize what they are giving up and appreciate the dedication. If no spouse, then a gift card to an outside interest that relaxes them prior to a stressful time.

#5: Care about developing me as a person … not just in words, but in actions. Invest in my/my team's growth and development. Agree to have mentors for me, coaches who believe in me and my strengths and help me understand what is required to get to the next level. If I don't meet your expectations, make sure the expectations are communicated to me clearly; I need to make sure I fully understand them, and give me the chance to fix it.

So many places say they develop and grow, but then never promote from within. Invest in your people. Give them the opportunity and reason to want to stay. Build on their strengths.

#4: Know that I would love to offer more than the job I am currently doing. Believe in me. Encourage me to use my brain and expand and grow. Each morning when I wake up I want to be excited and challenged by going to work. Help me in developing strategy plans so I can contribute more to the company.

Strong leaders I have worked with hold think tanks, pushing the team to create the future.

#3: Look at all of us in your company as extended members of your family. We want you to be successful, too. But please don't forget us along the way. We really do care about you, about the success of our company. If we feel a part of it, we will move mountains to make it successful.

Have you seen leaders who, upon retiring, turn the company over to their employees? It's because they became a work family. The team was so vested in the company, it was an extension of family.

#2: Recognize my strengths. Let me utilize the areas I am best in and be able to help the company in the best ways I can.

Leaders who focus on strengths to let their staff achieve have higher-energy staff members, more engaged members, fewer call-offs, and more focus and commitment.

#1: Remember what it was like when you were in our shoes, to be the worker bee beginning your career. How hurt you felt when not acknowledged, when you didn't feel part of the team, when a positive note from the boss or an executive would have motivated you to leap tall buildings. Never forget where you came from, and more importantly, how you got there and the feelings you had along the way. If you remember that, you will be a tremendous leader, and I promise we will do whatever it takes to make you and the company successful.

These are the leaders who have kept their notebook all these years, the book of what they liked in leaders and what they didn't like. These are the leaders who took their growth seriously and knew that someday they would have the opportunity to build great teams.

POTATO CHIP LEADERSHIP SKILLS

LEADERSHIP HOMEWORK

#1. Homework: Practice assessment

1. Make a list of your traits in dealing with your staff as you see them

2. Be honest as to how you deal with them

3. How many are negative traits?

4. List your team members' traits as you see them

5. How many are negative and how many are positive?

6. Which negative traits do you contribute to?

#2. Homework: Practice increasing your value to your team

1. List what you can do to improve yourself and the steps it will take to make it happen

#3. Homework: Practice positivity

1. Every day for a week at work and home start a conversation on a positive note

#4. Homework: Practice collaborative thinking

1. For the next two weeks as you need to make a team decision, ask for input from your team and listen carefully

#5. Homework: Practice "wow" moments with your team

1. Plan an experience that will create a memory for your staff

#6. Homework: Practice appreciation

1. Every day, sincerely compliment someone around you in front of other people

#7. Homework: Practice communication

1. Evaluate how you emailed/said things today

2. How would I have wanted to hear it if I were in that person's shoes?

#8. Homework: Practice knowing your team as a total person

1. Do I know what each of my staff members' outside goals and interests are?

2. How can I encourage them to reach that goal or participate in those interests?

#9. Homework: Practice humility

1. Who helps me be successful? (Remember: you're only as good as those around you)

2. Publicly pass along credit to as many as you can

#10. Homework: Practice letting go and giving ownership

1. Find a project you have that you can delegate.

2. Clearly communicate expectations and timeline and then let go

#11. Homework: Practice setting your team up for success

1. Go through your staff and list specific things you can do to help them succeed and achieve

2. Coach them through their game plan and help them prepare for success

#12. Homework: Practice listening

1. Put your phone down and step away from your computer

2. Engage your team member exclusively

3. Listen to what they are saying and have an uninterrupted conversation

#13. Homework: Practice celebrating

1. Every day a staff member hits a goal or goes above and beyond, leave a note or an afterhours voicemail, and reach out to your leader to do the same

#14. Homework: Practice celebrating Rock Star status

1. Each day, acknowledge someone who has done a great job as the Rock Star of your day

#15. Homework: Practice celebrating your people

1. Plan a yearly gathering for your team and their family, whether it's a cookout, an amusement park day, etc. Celebrate them as people. Create family.

www.ingramcontent.com/pod-product-compliance
Lightning Source LLC
Chambersburg PA
CBHW021139090426
42740CB00008B/858